WIL OF GOD

Embracing the Relentless Love
of a Special Child

Carrie Wilson Link

To all the angels in our lives

Carrie Wilson Link

ACKNOWLEDGMENTS

To properly thank everyone who has somehow touched my life, Wil's life, and inevitably this book, would take up more pages than the following story. We count among our many blessings the community that embraces our son, and a village that grows bigger every day. I must, however, thank my family and friends for their support and permission to tell what is really a collective experience. In particular, thank you to my husband, "Ed," for giving his blessing to put this story out into the world, despite his preference for privacy.

Thank you to "Jane" for being the daughter she is, the sister she is, and the impressive human she is, largely because of her ability to embrace what has not been an easy role for her. At this point Jane is considering becoming a therapist for siblings of special needs kids. There could be none greater.

Thank you to liz lieberg for encouraging me to start a blog, and being one of my biggest fans, and certainly, one of Wil's.

I appreciate all the love and support from my faithful blog followers. I feel your love come straight through the ether, and I am bolstered by it.

Thank you to Hope Edelman for taking a look at the first twenty pages of this book and writing the magical words, "You've got what it takes." That encouraged me to write on, persevere, and continue with this labor of love.

Thank you to Patty Giacchino for holding my feet to the fire, and reminding me for years, despite all the twists and turns my writing took me on, that the story to write was the one about Wil. She helped give it its name and certainly helped to give it wings.

In this lifetime I have always been blessed with good friends. Never was that more the case than during this long and often times discouraging process. Thank you to those that continued to ask, "How's your book?" and make me feel like God's gift to memoir: Susan True, Laurie Garrett, Meghan

Collins and Candace Primack.

My agent, Laurie Harper, became my greatest advocate and a life-long friend. Many times I thought to myself, *This book was worth writing if for no other reason than I got to know Laurie.* To have someone champion you the way she has me, has been incredible. Her belief in both the book and me sustained me. I especially appreciate that she felt, and conveyed, that the book was "moving, meaningful, wonderful, and worthy."

Thank you to Deb Shucka, Kari O'Driscoll, Val Hornburg, and Julie Pratt for reading earlier literary stabs, and believing in me.

Kim Meisner worked with me for years on several versions of books that were never born, but parts of which inevitably found their way into this book. It is fair to say this book could not have happened without her. She taught me so much about writing, but even more about life and love.

A special thanks to my friends who went through the book in its infancy, and then told me how great it was: Kerstin Maroney, Jen Holcomb, and Michelle O'Neil. You handled my "baby" with care, and I'll always be grateful.

There are three people who have had to listen to every little detail of this book and others, year after year. They patiently endured my foray into the world of a writer, then held up the mirror and showed me the way back when I got off course of what really mattered. They never judged and always loved. My love and thanks go to Terry Whitaker, Nancy Brown, and my side-by-side walking buddy for thirteen years, Kathleen Gianotti.

AUTHOR'S NOTE

This is a true story. I changed a handful of names, but to the best of my knowledge, ability, and integrity, everything happened just the way it's portrayed in the book. I am, however, both human and menopausal.

Carrie Wilson Link

INTRODUCTION

I ran to the drugstore today to pick up a prescription. I marched up to the counter and heard a woman to my left say, "Actually, there's a line." She was an elderly woman, sitting on the nearby bench waiting for the pharmacist to finish her order.

"Oh, okay, I'll stand over here and wait until you're done," I told her.

She took a harder look at me and said, "Aren't you the mother of the miracle boy?"

I had recognized her, too, but didn't know her name - knew she was what we call one of the "holy elders" at our church. When I donate blood she often checks me in.

"So, you were at his Baptism, I see."

"Yes, I've never seen anything like it," she said, "and I've seen a lot."

Then the woman proceeded to well up with tears and say, "That moment he raised his arms and led us all in the 'Alleluia Chorus,' really got me, it gets me just thinking about it."

"Yes, he's a special boy, alright," I said.

"He certainly is," she said, wiping her eyes.

Then I, the mother of the miracle boy, wiped my eyes, too.

FIRST NOBLE TRUTH:

There is suffering

CHAPTER ONE

It's 7:00 PM. Ed and I are in front of the TV watching an old "Seinfeld" episode. "It's not a lie if you believe it," George tells Jerry – letting him in on the big secret of how George has lived with himself all these years. I look over at Ed lying on the futon. He looks at me, too. It's one of our most repeated lines from "Seinfeld." It has become part of our code, our shorthand, our system for talking about people, but mostly it's our way of calling each other out. "It's not a lie…" I say to him when he tells me for the millionth time, "Stop buying ice cream, I'm going on a diet." He doesn't need to go on a diet, and that's not a lie.

We laugh our way through back-to-back "Seinfeld" episodes, eat our bowls of Dryer's, and then flip through the channels looking for something else to watch. Not finding anything exciting, Ed gets "the look" in his eye. I know the look, but I pretend I don't see it – yet.

"We want two kids, right?" he says. And even though we've never had that exact conversation before we both know we've been operating under that principle, that yes, we would eventually have two kids. I've always wanted two kids, maybe even three. I don't know why I've been reluctant to discuss this more with Ed, probably has something to do with the fact that we weren't exactly trying when I got pregnant with Jane, so to me, the subject of when and if we want more kids is a little touchy.

"Yea," I say, "eventually."

"Tonight is 'eventually,'" Ed says.

Quickly I do the math. "But that would mean a July baby, and July is your busiest time at work, and it's hot, and it's hard for summer babies when it comes to starting school, they're either the youngest or the eldest, and…" I'm stalling and I know it. I also know I will give in, and I will not be sorry. There is a part of me that believes there are no accidents. If we are supposed to conceive another baby and tonight is the night, so be it. That's how I felt about Jane – I just sensed her trying to make her way to us. I heard her from far away. Maybe Ed is hearing our next child now.

"Nobody gets pregnant the first time they try anyway," he says, already up off the futon, turning off lights, shutting the doors to the armoire and hiding the TV.

"I don't want to have another baby just because there wasn't anything good on TV tonight."

"Nobody gets pregnant the first time they try," he repeats.

It's not a lie if you believe it.

"One more big push," the doctor orders. "Push up, up to heaven, try *that*," she says, and I do. I try that. And it works. My epidural that I got shortly after we arrived at 1:00 PM is still working beautifully four hours later.

"It's a boy!" she says, and although I've known for all my thirty-three years I'd have a boy, known this baby was a boy from before he was conceived, it's still nice to hear. We chose not to find out the gender of either of our kids before their appearance – it's better that way, we believe. We also didn't do any of the optional testing – no amniocentesis, no genetic testing, nothing that wasn't required. Our feeling is that when you decide you're ready to make a baby that's the end of the decision making process – come what, and whom, may be.

Nicer even than hearing he's a boy is hearing him cry. A nice, lusty, full-term, healthy-baby cry. A cry we didn't hear right away with Jane, and both Ed and I get teary eyed when we hear this lovely sound now.

"And he's *huge*," the nurse says, placing him on my distended belly, wiping off the little blood that's on him. "Here," she says, handing Ed the special scissors, "do you want to cut the cord?" Ed nods and the nurse places the scissors awkwardly in his hand.

"Here?" he asks, scissors pointing about six inches from Wil's navel.

"That's perfect," she says. And Ed makes cuts through the center of what has tied his son and his wife together for nine months. The nurse clamps the end of Wil's umbilical cord and the doctor comes back to me, preparing me for the part nobody thinks about, the anticlimax - delivery of the placenta.

With a couple more good pushes the placenta is dispelled and just like that Wil is completely out of my body and into the world. We are separate now. Dual. Where once we were one. This makes me cry. When you're pregnant you are doing everything for two, but you are one. One mouth feeds two bodies. One thought affects who-knows-what. One experience is shared. Profoundly. How will we move through life in two different bodies when at my core I know we will forever be one?

One.

"It's a miracle, isn't it?" Ed asks, seeing my tears. And yes, it's a miracle, and yes I'm happy, and yes, I'm thrilled this baby is healthy, but there is a sadness. His survival is not just up to me anymore. He is part of this world.

I must share him with others. I must give him to the world.

"Does this baby have a name?" the doctor asks. She's not my regular doctor. She's the one on call this Sunday evening and is herself seven months pregnant with her second child. It shows, too, that she is a woman who has given birth once, and soon will again. She is gentle in her ways, a kindred spirit, with a soft approach I find very reassuring and comforting.

"Wil," both Ed and I say at the same time.

With the naming of Jane there is still some debate. Ed says I chose the name before he had fully agreed and there is a bit of truth to that. I loved the name Jane and filed it away years ago when Ed started talking about his cousin Jane in England. Loved the English ties, as we are both mostly English by heritage, loved the old-fashioned feel of it. Loved the strong, clean, simple sound of it. This baby, however, has been Wilson—Wil—for a long, long time. Forever. I remember clearly standing in my aunt's kitchen probably twenty years ago, talking to my cousin Julie. "When I have a son, I am going to name him Wilson," I stated, "I will call him Wil."

It's one hundred and three degrees outside but inside my hospital room it's a pleasant seventy-two. Wil lies in the crook of my arm, sleeping after nursing successfully for the first time. The nurses bring me ice bags for below and heating pads for my abdomen. Ed has gone home to be with Jane. I'm being waited on hand and foot. Wil is eating and sleeping like a pro. This is heaven and I never want to leave.

I remember those first couple of weeks after Jane was born. Everything made me cry, overwhelmed me - threw me for a loop. I was sore, tired, unbalanced in every way. How was I going to do all that again, this time with a two-year-old, as well?

About 4:30 PM the next day, Ed drives back to get Wil and me. I've asked him to bring me different clothes for Wil because he is so much bigger than the doctor predicted. The doctor thought Wil would be about seven and a half pounds, but Wil is nine pounds five ounces and twenty-three inches long, heavier and longer than Jane was at three months. I'd brought clothes for a newborn and there is no way they're going to fit him.

I am all business and have been for quite some time, at least since my dad got put on Hospice and his last months overlapped with my pregnancy. I have not sat down and had a good cry. I have not fallen apart. When I got the call from my brother Michael telling me Dad had died, I shed a tear or two, made the calls necessary to take care of Jane for the day, and prepared myself to get to Eugene with efficiency and speed taking precedence over emotions. Perhaps I was simply numb.

Ed loads me into the wheelchair, Wil on my lap, our suitcase hanging from Ed's arm and away we go, out into the heat, out into the real world, out into our lives. And into Ed's car that gets a flat tire a mile down the road.

My Principal, Ken, warned me when I went into his office last winter to tell him I was pregnant and due in July: Having two kids is far, far harder than one. "Don't worry," I said, I will be back for my one-day-a-week job in September. Six weeks will be enough time to recover.

"You'll be glad to get away one day a week!" he said. "Two kids is not twice as hard as one, it's six times harder."

I teach talented and gifted kids. It has worked great for the past two years, ever since I left my full-time teaching job after Jane was born. I take Jane to Ed's parents' house, just a couple miles from where I teach and they play with her all day. It will be a little trickier with two kids. I may ask them to come here to our house, instead, since taking them both there would mean that I have to figure out how to get all three of us dressed and ready by 7:00 AM, a task that seems insurmountable at this point.

Jane's not potty trained yet; she just turned two, two months ago. Wil is two weeks old and it's at least 10:00 AM before we ever get out the door. Wil pees every time I take off his diaper. Boys are a whole different breed – he sprays the ceiling, everything we're both wearing and the entire dining room table we're using as a changing table since there is no room in this house for one extra piece of furniture. The table isn't even under the dining room light. It's pushed way over by the wall so we can squeeze by to get to the kitchen. By the time I successfully change Wil, throw whatever he and I were both wearing into what I'm now calling Mount Laundry, change Jane's diaper and change my own "supplies," it's about time to start all over again.

Jane is a good girl, but she is two. She can talk, she can walk, but what I have her doing most of the time is sitting in front of an endless reel of "Sesame Street" that I've recorded. She eats bowl after bowl of Goldfish cheddar cheese crackers and bottle after bottle of 2% milk. Feeding her a proper meal is a thing of the past. I can hardly remember standing in the kitchen cutting fresh fruit and vegetables up for her in small chunks so she wouldn't choke, but would be properly fed.

I change Jane's diaper, then Wil's, then check myself for leakage. I put fresh pads over my swollen breasts, check the diaper bag for wipes, pacifiers, extra cloth diapers and wraps, snacks for Jane, pads for me, burp rags, and was just ready to go when Wil, in his infant seat next to me, starts to scream. I pull him out of the seat and stick him on the boob before finding a clear place on the futon for me to sit down, wearily. Wil on one breast, my hand pressing firmly over the other to keep it from squirting across the room, my milk lets down and with it so does the blood. I feel the inadequacy of my "feminine protection."

"Jane?" I say, breaking her trance from "Sesame Street."
"Will you please bring me the phone?" Jane scoots to the end of the rocking chair, jumps the rest of the way down, toddles over to the phone sitting on its base in the kitchen and brings it to me. At two, she is just getting hair, soft, blond flyaway tufts I've tried to hold back in a plastic pink clip. She speaks with her pacifier, "fafa," still in her mouth. (She calls it a fafa, of course, because I loudly and repeatedly proclaimed to the universe that no child of mine, nor I, would substitute any silly words for pacifier. We would call it what it was -- we were that kind of family.)

"Here, Mommy," she says, handing me the phone.
"Jill?" I say when she answers the phone, "we are going

to be late. I'm feeding Wil again, then I'll have to change all our diapers again, then he'll need to eat again, then I'll need to change all our diapers again, and eventually, we'll be over there."

Jill assures me she understands and I know she does. She has two kids of her own; she has been here...right in the middle of hell.

The phone rings right after I hang up with Jill and I think it must be her calling back, so I grab it while still nursing Wil. It is not Jill. It is my deceased father's attorney in Eugene calling to remind me of my responsibilities. There are papers that need signatures, there are forms to be faxed, there are things to mail and IRS reports to file. There are accountants to call. There are realtors to hire, houses to sell, properties to improve and seventy-four years of what can loosely be described as a life, to clean up.

My father died five weeks ago. I am the executor of his will. I am overwhelmed with the details that closing down a seventy-four-year-old partially lived life entails, but I can't think about any of that now. I finish feeding Wil and put him down in his infant seat, the one that rocks if you put your foot on it and jiggle.

I get up off the futon, gingerly make it to the bathroom, freshen up and take a quick look in the mirror. Not good. I look as bad and as tired as I feel.

But right now, all I want is to stop Wil's screaming that has started back up in the three minutes I had to myself. *There is no way that child is hungry*, I think to myself, *so what in the hell is he crying about?* It feels like Wil was born happy and then about two weeks later he started screaming. It's a blur now, I can't even remember... were there two weeks where I had this situation under control? I consider finding paper and pencil and writing down all my notes from the attorney phone call before I forget but the screaming is urgent, so I pick up Wil, infant carrier and all, and grabbing the two plastic blue handles, I start to swing.

Wil's screams are downgraded to a cry, and I think, *"Oh!*

He just needed a little movement, that's all, no problem, I can do that."

Six diapers and a full episode of "Sesame Street" later, the three of us are out the door, and headed out. I have it in my head that going over to Jill's will be great, that letting Jane play with Jill's two little boys will be fun for her, and besides, I see mothers with their newborns in car seats hanging from the bottom of their sagging arms all the time, how hard can it be?

I take a quick look at my watch and see that it is already noon. Now we'll have to hurry to be back for Jane's nap, otherwise she'll fall asleep in the car on the way home from Jill's, never make the transfer to her bed, and the rest of the day will be ruined. If I don't get her nap time, I'll never have dinner ready for Ed when he gets home at 5:00. It is part of the goal, part of the dream, part of the expectation that I put on myself to have a healthy dinner ready every night when he walks in the door. After all, I'm a stay-at-home mother and he's busy working. It should be my job to feed him, and besides, maybe if I cook for him, I'll remember to eat myself.

We're just leaving Jill's; I've got Jane by the hand and am almost to my car when I hear Jill say with a laugh, "Did you want to take your son, too?" I look up at the 1920's bungalow and see Jill standing there smiling, holding Wil in his car seat in her manicured hand. I hate Jill right now. I hate that she makes it all look so easy. I hate that during the hour we just spent at her house not a thing was out of place. She was showered, her boys had on clean clothes, and worse…she seemed happy. I hate that Jane wouldn't leave my side to go play. I hate that Wil screamed almost the whole time, and the only way I could get him to stop was to swing him in the car seat. But mostly, I hate that Jill has just busted me for being the world's worst mother. Who forgets their newborn son?

We climb into the Corolla; I start the engine, push in "Wee Sing Bible Songs" again, and make a vow right then and there: I will never ever forget again, not even for one second, that I am not just the mother of one child, but of two.

CHAPTER TWO

Ed's mom Doreen and his sister Jenelle gave me a double stroller for a baby shower gift. They shopped for weeks before selecting a navy blue and white one with a seat for Jane in the front and a place in the back that can convert to a seat or lay down flat for a baby. Most days I put Jane in the front with her fafa, pink bear in her lap and pink crocheted blanket, "Fossie," wrapped around her shoulders like a stole. I put Wil in the back with his fafa and we walk down to the end of our street, around the corner and to the "Little Store." It has a real name, but everyone in the neighborhood calls it the Little Store. Sometimes I just need stamps. Sometimes I just need cash and know that I can write a check for over the amount of whatever I spend, and don't have to pack both kids in the car to drive to the bank. Sometimes we just need to get out of the house and this is usually successful.

In the short walk to the store or in the store itself, we inevitably run into neighbors who know we've just moved into the neighborhood and have two children. "Which school are you going to do?" they ask. We're not here a month before I can see the neighborhood is clearly drawn down the middle by invisible and not necessarily religious lines; between those choosing the local and reputably good public school, and the K-8 Catholic school.

"We haven't decided yet," I say, at the same time thinking, *I have a two-year-old and an infant, do I really need to know right this minute?* But we sort of do know, and that all went into our decision to move to this neighborhood and into this tiny house while we build a bigger one. While still living in Northeast Portland, we had wandered around the local Catholic grade school in that neighborhood, going so far as to put Jane's name on a kindergarten waiting list three years out. We'd heard good things about the Catholic school and now there's one a short walk up the street from where we are living and where we are planning to build.

My first two years of teaching were at a Catholic grade school here in Portland. Having gone to a Catholic high school, most of my friends were Catholic, many of whom I'd gone to Mass with. I knew my way around the Catholic services pretty well, but was not official. Ruth, my best friend from high school and I had been roommates in college and then again out of college, both earning teaching degrees and very little money. She found a job in a Catholic grade school right out of college, but I did not find a teaching job so I worked at Nike for a couple of years. One summer day, Ruth said, "Carrie, we have a new principal and a teacher opening at my school. You should call and ask if you can apply."

I called, made an appointment for an interview and went in later that week. Terry, the principal, was a big, casual, kind man with two small children. He'd just gotten the job, having left a struggling Catholic school nearby. He'd agreed to be the principal as well as teach two periods a day of grades sixth through eighth. "We're looking for someone to teach mostly sixth grade. We have a teacher that will teach the seventh/eighth grade split, and I will teach a little of all three grades. You would teach the writing and reading to all three grades and be the homeroom for the sixth graders. Are you interested?"

I could tell I had the job if I wanted it. "Well," I said, "I'm not actually Catholic. Is that a problem? I can fake my way through the Mass, I'm fine teaching religion and don't have a problem with Catholicism, but I just wanted you to know the truth."

"Let's just make that our little secret," he said. And that's how it came to be that I taught in a Catholic school for two years without ever telling any of the teachers, students or parents that I was a fraud.

Although that school paid me so little money I could not afford to keep teaching there and the next year I moved to a third and fourth grade split, effectively teaching five grades in two years, I gained tremendous respect for the way the Catholics educate their children - their culture of education. And not enough could be made of the K-8 model to my way of thinking. I loved how the older kids had responsibilities in the school: setting up for assemblies, helping in the cafeteria, yard work outside. I loved the buddy classrooms where younger kids read and were mentored by the older kids. I loved how the junior high kids were kept in the same building with their younger siblings and were expected to be role models, not set adrift in a school with only other kids their age. The whole middle school/junior high model never made sense to me. I didn't like it as a student, I didn't like it as a student teacher, and now as a parent I didn't want it for my children.

While teaching at that little school, I worked with a woman named Janet. The first time Ed saw Janet's house he said, "Tell her we'll buy her house if she ever wants to sell it." As it turned out, a few years later she got divorced and needed to sell her house. We had her come up with a fair price and we bought it from her, as is. That is the house that became our rental. That is the house that we moved into after my dad died and before Wil was born. That is the house we live in right now, the tiny one that holds us as we build a bigger one next door.

Maybe that was why I needed to work at that struggling little Catholic school all those years ago: to meet Janet. To see the beauty of Catholic education. To have the answer to the question, "Where are you going to send your kids?"

Thank God it's summer and it stays light so long because that means I can take Wil to Fred Meyer at 9:00 at night and still have daylight. On the other hand, maybe if it would darken earlier this kid could get his circadian rhythms figured out and we could all catch some sleep. Fred Meyer is your one-stop shopping center. Their jingle is, "What's on your list today? You'll find it at Fred Meyer," and that's pretty much true. Maybe I'll find my sanity there, too.

"It's just colic, right?" I ask the doctor at Wil's two-week check-up. "It'll pass?"

The doctor smiles at me, bobs his prematurely grey head full of hair, and I can tell he's humoring me. And I want to be humored. I want humor, at any cost. Nothing is funny about this situation. Nothing. Since our car got that flat tire on the way home from the hospital and woke Wil from his newborn recovery sleep, he's been awake and crying ever since. No, crying isn't the right word for it; it's much more of a scream than a cry, a bloody murder scream, a scream that makes a person do desperate things just to get the crying to stop.

"So, three months and it will go away? That's how long colic lasts, right?" I again ask the doctor.

"That's usually the case, yes," he assures me, but I can tell he knows nothing at all.

"Isn't there anything I can *do* to make him stop?" I plead.

"Most of the 'treatments' for colic are really just to make the parent feel better, give them something to do. There really isn't anything that helps except time."

When I recount the information to my friends, they call foul on every level.

"You can watch what you eat – eliminate all the foods that make you and him gassy!"

"Try Mylicon," one suggested.

"Peppermint," another said, "Just a drop diluted in water and put that in a bottle for him to drink."

But nothing I do works. Just to get him out of the house and let Jane and Ed get some sleep, I put him in his infant carrier, load him into the Toyota, blast the air conditioner, "Wee Sing Bible Songs" and drive. I played this tape for Jane the whole time I was pregnant. I truly believe Wil fell in love with the songs, and possibly God, then. "He's Got the Whole World in His Hands," "The B-I-B-L-E," and "Michael Row Your Boat Ashore," play as we go. Most babies fall asleep in the car. Not this baby. The car was just a vehicle for getting the two of us out of the house and to Fred Meyer where the aisles are wide and the faces anonymous. Putting his carrier in the center of the cart, I push that cart up and down the aisles, jogging behind it.

Wil doesn't like the jogging stroller. He doesn't like the infant swing and hates the rocking chair. They all just rile him up more. He likes *real* movement, not some ridiculous soothing activity.

And so, night after night, we fly through Fred Meyer's and I get the looks. But the looks have stopped bothering me because I am giving off my own looks, looks that say to these strangers, "Do you have a *better* idea? Because I'd really like to see you *try*."

Four other stay-at-home moms with toddlers and babies are going out to dinner tonight, and they've invited me. "I have to bring Wil," I explain.

"Really? You can't just leave him with Ed? For *one* night?"

"No. You don't get it. Wil cries. He doesn't stop. But if I nurse him and jiggle him, he turns the volume down. A little."

It doesn't seem fair to them. It doesn't seem fair to me either, but I can't leave Wil with Ed. I can't leave him with anyone except Ed's parents one day a week for seven hours and that's because there are two of them. I don't trust anyone else not to lose it with this kid, do something bad to him - hurt him in some way.

I don't even trust myself.

The restaurant is Italian, noisy. Everyone's drinking wine and loosening up. From what I can hear of the snippets of conversation, they're all having a nice time. I, on the other hand, am up out of my seat jumping up and down with Wil, my boob in his mouth, my belly fat bouncing for anyone to see who cares enough to look.

I don't care. I need out of my house, these women are my friends and I deserve to be here as much as these people, all trying to have a good time. Finally though, after an hour of bouncing, jumping, boobing – shoving my boob in his mouth at every opportunity - and partial conversations, I go home.

I strap Wil safely into his car seat in the back, crank on the air conditioner, turn up the Bible songs and I sit in that parking lot and cry. It's hard to say which one of us was crying louder tonight.

Wil is two months old today. I dress him in his Hanna Anderson little green two-piece outfit that is so comfy looking it might as well be pajamas. I want this boy to be comfortable. "He is still really colicky," I tell Dr. Miller, our family practitioner, as if the constant crying needs explanation. "I'm worried he's going to be a fussy baby forever, maybe just an unhappy child in general."

Dr. Miller puts a hand through his long, wavy, thick grey hair, smiles in a comforting way and says, "There is no connection between his unhappiness now and the future nature of your boy."

I am comforted to hear this but still have a strong sense that something much bigger is wrong with my child than just colic. At the same time, something drops deep when I hear Dr. Miller's words: if this boy is happy someday, that will be enough. That will be more than enough. That will be everything.

"I am reading *What to Expect the First Year* and looking through Jane's old baby books. His development is off, don't you think? Shouldn't he be rolling over one way by now? The book says he should. And what about following an object in an arc past the midline? He's not doing that, either. He's not reaching for objects. He's not making any sounds at all except crying, and he doesn't lift up his head when he's on his stomach."

I hand Goldfish crackers to Jane, then a sippy cup, and try to keep her from falling off the doctor's spinning stool that she insists on sitting on. I have redressed Wil and am holding him on my chest, jumping up and down like a pogo stick.

"And what about *this?*" I ask Dr. Miller. "Look how hard and fast I have to jump to make him stop crying. He doesn't like to be soothed the way Jane did, he likes to be jostled!"

"That's just the difference between a boy and a girl," Dr. Miller says.

It's not a lie, if you believe it.

Today is Wil's first birthday. I baked a cake in the shape of a cowboy boot, dyed some of the frosting yellow and the rest brown, and made a big dinner for the whole family. My mom, "Grammy," brought him a balloon with Sesame Street characters on it that says "For Baby's First Birthday." He seems interested in it – probably from all the "Sesame Street" that's on TV all the time around here.

I'm trying to get Wil to drink from a cup but either he can't or he won't. He will drink bottle after bottle of whole milk, however. I'm not having to shake him to sleep as much anymore, some nights I can even get him to fall asleep on his own by just putting his fafa in his mouth and laying him on his back in the crib. About one to three times a night he cries and I have to go back in and find the fafa and put it back in his mouth. Why don't they make those things glow-in-the-dark? I would invent that myself if I had the time.

He's reaching for things – usually with his left hand – so we think he'll be left-handed. He picks up food from his high chair with this left hand, too. He's doing a tiny bit of crawling but drags his left leg then hoists his right leg along – it's weird. I'm worried that he's not creeping or walking or even crawling in the conventional sense. It seems like he should be. He's not really responding to one-step commands like the word "No" either, even if you gesture.

What he does like to do is open the cupboard doors back and forth, especially the lower cupboards of the armoire that hold the stereo. Then he moves the knobs on the stereo so when you turn it on you about blast your eardrums out.

I take Wil in for his one-year well check and told the doctor my concerns that he's still not saying any words or trying to walk. Again, the doctor is not concerned, or if he is, he sure isn't acting like it. He wants me to come back in three months and see how Wil's doing then.

Today is Wil's fifteen-month well check and I've voiced all my concerns to Dr. Miller who says, "Wil is slower to develop than average but not abnormally so. I want you to bombard him with words. He needs to hear language even if he doesn't give it back."

"But we *do* that," I insisted. "We talk all the time and I try to read him books. He just grabs the pages and closes them. He doesn't like it."

I really like Dr. Miller. He has two kids the same ages as ours and he's super nice, but there's something about him that tells me he's just not getting it. It's great that he's not in a panic, but I would appreciate it if he didn't make me feel like I'm over-reacting.

At Wil's eighteen-month well-check he's still not walking. He's still not talking. He is still crying, all the time. Dr. Miller says, "He is where you'd expect a twelve-month old to be, but a six month delay isn't extraordinary. It could just be caused by having an older sister who does everything for him. However, I can give you the name of a specialist if you'd like."

I'd like.

CHAPTER THREE

I don't know if I want the specialist to find anything going on or not. I just want the crying to stop. I want the walking to start. I want the communication to expand so that what this child wants and needs can somehow be communicated to me, and I can somehow respond appropriately. I would also like to expand my own coping skills to more than the oft repeated, "God, Wil," when he gets going and I can't make him stop. With my luck, he is going to go to first grade and say his first name is "God" and his middle name is "Wil."

Ed and I schedule our appointment with the Developmental Pediatrician at the local children's hospital. An Indian woman in a jewel-toned sari greets us warmly, takes Wil in her arms and explains she's Dr. Budden, won't we please follow her? *Dr. Budden, if you can tell me what's wrong with my child, I will follow you to the ends of the earth,* I think to myself as we walk the halls back to her examining room.

I don't know what I was expecting, but this isn't it. After eighteen head banging months of nobody taking my concerns seriously, this gift from India begins to diagnose faster than my hand can take notes.

"He is a super-pronator – no wonder he's not walking – orthotics, he needs orthotics."

"He has a big head – he is one of those big headed kids." Ed and I just looked at each other as if it to say, "What?"

"Poor muscle tone.

"Weak core strength.

"His eyes aren't working together.

"Sensory system is off.

"Adenoids are huge – does he snore?"

On and on she went, and yes and yes, we nodded and nodded. Our heads swam and my fingers cramped from writing everything down.

"Call Portland Early Intervention Program – PeiP -when you get home – get going on this – the sooner the better."

Her words, "Call PeiP," rang in my head – a fire alarm. I knew two families in PeiP and their kids had serious issues, issues anyone could see. Was I joining those ranks? Would making that phone call seal that deal? Would denial keep me out of that "club"? What was the cost of that membership? What was the cost of not joining?

I wanted to both hug her and kill her, simultaneously. Finally someone was validating my concerns, and I had every right to have them – in fact, it turns out, I hadn't had enough. And nobody had listened to me. Now was it too late? Had we already thrown away eighteen precious months, never to recover them?

We endured one and a half hours of this, picked up our baby at the end of it and went home. All I felt like doing when I got home was drinking. Heavily. But I got busy. Drinking isn't my thing, anyway – sure, a beer or glass of wine now and then, but that's about it. Even if my father hadn't been an alcoholic and even if I hadn't received all the warnings of how easily children of alcoholics become one, too, that's not what I do in times of stress.

I'm getting the kids ready for bed about a week later with Jane in the bathtub and Wil jammied and in my arms when the phone rings.

"Hi, Carrie? This is Dr. David Willis. I'm a Behavioral/Developmental Pediatrician. Your name was recently given to me by a fellow pediatrician, Dr. Budden. She thought your family might be a good fit for a project I'm working on. I'm bringing world-renowned Developmental Pediatrician, Dr. Stanley Greenspan to Portland. From what Dr. Budden tells me, your son would be ideal for what we're trying to do: To watch over time the recovery process of highly unregulated toddlers and how they respond to what Dr. Greenspan calls 'Floor-Time.'"

I didn't know at the time that this was code for: your child is seriously messed up, and we need to pull out all the stops.

Floor-Time is also code for: We think your kid is autistic, but we don't want to say it. After so long looking for answers and help, I had more answers and help than I could manage. I told Dr. Willis we'd think about it. I got Jane out of the tub and into bed. I got Wil out of my arms and onto his side of the twin bed we shared in the attic — as far away from Ed and Jane as possible so his nightly shrieks would only keep one of us awake, instead of three. Then I laid down next to him, looked deeply into his ocean-blue eyes that apparently didn't work together properly, and said, "We'll get through this, my son. So help me, God." And for the first time, but not the last, not by a long shot, I thought of the Virgin Mary, and understood that whole "You and me against the world" thing she and Jesus had going on.

Because that's how it felt - Wil and me on one side, Ed, Jane and the rest of the world on the other. Deep within me is a knowing that that's not the case, I know that Ed is on Wil's side, definitely, and certainly on mine, too. However, there is something about being Wil's mother that separates me from Wife of Ed, Mother of Jane. There is a phenomenon taking place I cannot name nor understand, but feel at a cellular level. It feels important. It feels old. It feels divine. And it feels scary as hell.

My days are one long blur of brushing, compressing, speech, physical, occupational and social therapy. We were taught by the occupational therapist something called "brushing," where after stripping him down to his diaper, I take a small, white surgical brush and rub it all over Wil's body in a specified way: not too lightly and not too harshly. What follows is something called joint compressions, which entails taking every joint in every finger, toe, shoulder, elbow, wrist, knee and ankle, and pushing each in and out a few times. We do this every two hours when he's awake and he is always awake.

Because our boy is under three, the Early Intervention therapists come to our home. I welcome them like long lost brothers and sisters. Some adults to talk to. Some adults to help. Some adults to truly understand. I don't know how much they help my son, but they keep me from "jumping" and that's saying something.

Together we roll him tightly in blankets and swing him like a hammock. The full body pressure awakens his sensory system. We gently bounce him on the bed to get him to make guttural vocalizations. Lying on his back, our hands on his shoulders, pressing playfully, to get the "ugh ugh ugh" sound, training his mouth to do more than cry. We stack cups and put body parts on Mr. Potato Head endlessly.

"Nose!" we say gleefully, while placing the nose on Mr. Potato Head.

"Nose!" we coo while touching his nose.

"Nose!" we sing while touching our own noses.

And so it goes, and goes and goes.

The boy has stopped crying constantly… after almost two full years and the talking has begun. The talking has begun and the underlying Obsessive Compulsive Disorder has come into the light. He finds something he loves and we speak of nothing else for days, sometimes weeks.

Wil has his favorite footy pajamas. They are white with navy blue trim around the neck. He's worn them so much that the feet are full of holes. Wherever those pajamas are he finds them, brings them to me, and wants to wear them. Because I am too vain to let him be seen in the ratty footy pajamas, but practical enough to know this isn't a battle worth fighting, we've compromised. I get him dressed for the day in a cute pair of pants or overalls and a clean, cute, matching top and he wears the pajamas like a cape. We put his little arms through and he drags the rest behind him.

Wil comes to me in his cape, holding Big Bird and requests, "Five!" We walk to the TV, push rewind for a couple seconds until it begins. He and Big Bird dance in front of the TV and when there's still three seconds left, he yells, "FIVE!" The video is actually called "Yo, Five" and has Elmo in a rapper outfit complete with leather pants and sunglasses. We watch "five," fifty-five times a day, it feels like.

Once Wil finally started walking, it wasn't long until he began to run. He's somewhat of an escape artist, too. We have those big, white plastic childproof devices on all the doorknobs to keep him from bolting out the door and getting hit by a car. It's almost more than I can comfortably grasp to put my hands around the childproof opener, squeeze the two grey dots on either side and carefully turn. Still, I live with fear and dread that he's going to get out and get hurt. I don't let him out of my sight.

"BLUE TWO!" he barks while trying in vain to open the door. When Jane is at preschool, I'm able to accommodate his latest obsession. I slip on the shoes that we keep in a basket by the door, get his shoes on, throw a coat over his clothes and jammie cape, and away we go.

I don't know how or when exactly he discovered blue twos. And I cannot possibly say why he's fascinated with them, other than he is. In Oregon, there are two places for stickers that you apply to your license plate after you renew with the DMV and DEQ. On the right you apply the last two digits of the year and on the left, the month in which the new tags expire. February is a blue sticker with a white two. The whole thing is no bigger than a one-and-a-half inch square.

We take off down the street and walk to where we have staked out all the blue twos. He barrels ahead while I silently pray, "Oh, please be home and have your car in the driveway so we can move on."

He runs so fast I am at my full speed to keep up with him. Sometimes I have to grab him by the cape just to make sure he isn't more than a foot ahead of me. We don't live on a busy street, but still there are cars and he seems to have no sense of danger. "Wil!" I shout, "car!" Either he doesn't notice or doesn't care. I'm not sure which. I think he has a number in his head of how many blue twos we have to see (and touch) before we come home, but he can't tell me this yet and I haven't cracked the code.

Jane goes to preschool on Mondays, Thursdays and Fridays. There is a local high school with a preschool right in it. It's great. Not only is it really inexpensive, but there's one-on-one attention from the high school students helping out for credit. There are two teachers, Claudia and Sandra. Claudia has brown hair and suffers from lupus. She is the teacher. Sandra has dyed auburn hair, big glasses, an even bigger laugh and is the assistant. Wil loves taking Jane to preschool and it's hard dragging him out after we get in the door. The only thing that works is I say, "Come on, Wil, it's time to go to Safeway!"

Safeway is our closest big grocery store. We go there for what we can't get at the Little Store, and for the blue twos in the parking lot. Wil follows me to the car, I buckle him into his car seat, hand him Big Bird and his fafa and plug in "Wee Sing Bible Songs." For fifteen minutes I let my mind wander and my shoulders relax.

It takes us fifteen to twenty minutes to get from the car to the building because we snake all through the rows of cars looking for blue twos. With each one he finds he shouts, "Blue two!" and I clap like a mad woman.

We walk into Safeway and he is greeted by name. "Hi, Wil!" shouts Larry from produce. "Hi, Wil!" shouts Marlies in lane two. "Hi, Wil!" shouts Lonnie in lane three. Carmen, Carla and Steve make sure to shout "hi," too, when we pass them on our way through the store looking for nothing in particular.

We've come to Safeway several days a week and it's a bit of a sanctuary for me. It's a little like "Cheers" -- a place where everyone knows my name, my story, and loves and accepts it. Wil is just Wil, the cute towheaded boy with a fafa in his mouth, wearing a jammie cape, and holding Big Bird.

CHAPTER FOUR

I do a good job of taking care of Jane. I get her dressed, fed, to and from preschool, and even manage to arrange play dates and take her places like the Children's Museum, the science museum and the zoo. I coordinate outings with other friends, we pack the car full of snacks and diapers, the backpack for me to put Wil in, and away we go. He cries, I reach backwards to shove bottles, Goldfish and fafas in his mouth and I pretend we're all having a fun time and I'm making lasting, meaningful memories for Jane. She shouldn't have to suffer more than she already does just because she has a high-maintenance brother. Her life should go on as normally as possible and I am determined to make that happen.

I remember when my cousin Julie was telling me about going from having one child to two. We were walking down the street on a beautiful Portland spring day, me several months pregnant, and she said, "When you have an only child, it's all about the child. When you have your second child, it's still all about the first one. You just make your second one mold to fit the schedule and demands of the one already there. By the time you have your third, you've got that younger kid napping in the car on the way to take the bigger kids places; things you would never have considered doing with the first one."

I think back on that conversation now and I see how hard I'm working to keep Jane in the number-one spot. But I'm already aware that Wil and his needs are going to take over, if they haven't already, and probably stay there. She was seventeen months old when I got pregnant and if I'm being honest with myself, she lost me from that moment on. First, to morning sickness and fatigue, then to insomnia and worry, then to the death of my father and subsequent responsibilities closing his estate.

We've just dropped Jane off at preschool, have already been to Safeway to see our friends and pick up a few groceries... I've even got Wil down for a nap. I back out slowly from the room he and Jane share, close the door, careful not to let it latch as that tiny sound is likely to wake him up and start the whole going to sleep rig-a-ma-roll again: fafa, bouncing on my hip, gently putting him down, tiptoeing out, avoiding all creaks and groans from the old house and all clicking of hardware. I walk through the kitchen, down the basement stairs and busy myself with laundry. I look at all the unsorted clothes on the floor. As I separate whites from darks and work to squirt all the stains and spills with Shout, my mind wanders back to the first time I realized Jane would never have the kind of attention from me that I had always dreamed of bestowing on my children – especially my first born.

In the summer of 1996, my seventy-four-year-old father died at home. Some say he died of emphysema. Some say he died from cirrhosis of the liver. I say he committed suicide in the most cowardly and selfish way possible: slowly.

My swollen belly kept me an uncomfortable distance from the steering wheel as I drove the two hours to Eugene from the home I shared with Ed and two-year-old Jane in Portland. I arrived at my father's home just hours after the attendees from the funeral parlor had removed his body. My brother Michael was living with my dad at the time – helping take care of him. Together, Michael and I made all the funeral arrangements, the burial decisions and contacted all the people who needed to know he had died. All three of them. When you've spent most of the last twenty years drinking and smoking in your kitchen, not a whole lot of people really need to hear you're not doing that anymore.

I waddled through my dad's house, heavy with resentment, heavy with responsibility – light on grief. I moved into his living room, which for the last few years served as a storeroom for the remnants of his dying legal career.

I looked through files, moving old, musty paper work until I found what I was looking for, his will. Eyes quickly scanned the relatively short document – five pages – and my fears were realized. He'd made me the executor.

Back at the drinking table, papers spread wide, my brother and I absorb the news. "The bastard's going to control me from the grave," Michael says. "And me, too," I add. This is no gift, no honor. This is a noose around my neck.

My eyes leave the papers in front of me and look out the sliding glass door at the view. The house is on a hill – College Hill, as Eugene is the home of the Oregon Ducks. While standing on the deck or sitting in the living room, or washing dishes in the kitchen, you can look out at South Eugene. There are trees, hills, schools and a minor league baseball team's field – the Emeralds, "Ems." The view is one of the reasons my dad bought this house nearly thirty years ago. I think it made him feel on top of the world. He could look at all that he ruled from this vantage point. And thirty years ago maybe he had a right to feel that way – he was married, at least on paper, he had a couple of cute kids and a promising career in politics. He was a state legislator and from the view out this window, he could see most of his district.

It was at this table that I had the last conversation with my dad before he died. "You know, you and Vanna White are due about the same time," he said with a look that said, "This is the best I can do. We can't talk about the fact that I'm dying. Let's talk about 'Wheel of Fortune,' please." I'm pretty sure he had more of a relationship with Vanna White than he ever thought of having with me so it's fitting that he knows this. Instead of saying that though, instead of getting into our usual argument, I just smiled and said, "You know? If this baby is a boy, we're going to name him Wilson – carry on the family name, and all that." What I didn't say, but his face told me he heard was, "And that is the best I can do."

My dad didn't respond. His mouth, face and soul remained behind a veil, giving me no indication as to how this announcement affected him or even if it did. I chose to believe it made him happy. I hope he saw it as a sign that I didn't resent everything about him.

Breaking from my reverie, I ask Michael, "So, who should officiate this funeral?"

"What would really set him off, but in a good way, would be to ask the priest that Hospice sent. He was great, and there's something so right about having a Catholic priest preside at Dad's death... since during his life, he hated all Catholics."

My brother and I are in full agreement.

It is hot for this early in June. Normally the Willamette Valley doesn't get its heat until the fifth of July -- it's almost a joke -- but heat has come today along with its friend, humidity.

I stand on the rolling lawn of the cemetery, one eye on the Catholic priest, Fr. Joe, who we've asked to do the service, one eye on my toddling daughter who wants out of her daddy's arms and into mine.

My young daughter's hair is blond and blowing. She's arms and legs, twisting and turning, trying to find a place within my hold. There is no place for her to rest comfortably with her unborn sibling already taking me farther and farther away from her.

"It's okay, honey, I've got you," I try to soothe while wondering if I've really "got her" whatsoever.

The breeze gives comfort to the small group. Of the few people gathered here, even fewer can say they really knew my father. Most of the people here are showing their support for me, for my brother Michael, and even my mom after all these years.

As I look briefly from the eyes of the priest to those of the group, steady figures in my life look back. My godparents/aunt and uncle have made the long drive over the Cascade Mountains from their home in Sisters, Oregon. My second mother -- my mom's sister -- is there. My closest cousin Julie dropped everything and came down from Seattle, over five hours away. These are the same people who continued to ask about my dad long after he disappeared from their lives, and thus, from my mom's side of the family. Now they stand in a semi-circle round the urn, darkly dressed, my uncle in a suit, the women wearing heels sinking into the recently watered lawn, eyes down, showing their respect. Perhaps they, like me, believed my dad had enough humanity that he was worth respecting upon his death. Perhaps they were willing to forgive and forget all the stories of drunkenness, hostility, manipulation and abandonment they'd heard so many times. Perhaps they were just there out of duty.

It seems wrong to wear casual sandals to your own father's funeral. It seems wrong to be swollen and pregnant, burying a man named Wilson, carrying his grandchild, possibly another Wilson. It seems wrong to see all these people that I know would rather be anywhere but here on this hot, miserable, heavy, heavy day.

Wrong. That's the right word for what this is.

Fr. Joe is wearing black pants, a short-sleeved black shirt and the white collar that identifies him as a man of the cloth. He moves his arms in the sign of the cross and says, "In the name of the Father, Son, and Holy Spirit," and even though there isn't a Catholic amongst us, we all say, "Amen."

And mean it.

WIL OF GOD

Carrie Wilson Link

THE SECOND NOBLE TRUTH:

Attachment is the cause of suffering

CHAPTER FIVE

Ed and I have been talking about the phone call from Dr. Willis. "Call your friend Kerstin," Ed says, "she might have good advice." Ed is right; Kerstin is deeply entrenched with Early Intervention. The next day, after I get Jane to preschool and Wil down for a nap, I go up into the attic with the cordless phone and whisper, so as not to disturb Wil, and call her.

"Dr. Willis is well-known in Oregon, Carrie," Kerstin tells me, "and Dr. Greenspan is really famous in the special needs world. He started what they call Floor Time. He's going to want to get you down on the floor with Wil and teach you how to engage him to bring him out of himself and into the world. It's what they do with kids they think are autistic."

"Nobody has used that word to describe Wil," I argue.

"Well, what are they calling him at PeiP?" she asks.

"DD – Developmentally Delayed," I say.

"Whatever they want to call it, they're going to teach you Floor Time. Floor Time is a *huge* time sucker. You're going to be doing Floor Time every day, all day long. Like you don't have enough to do already with the brushing therapy, speech/language, occupational and physical therapy!"

I know Kerstin is not just being grumpy. This is the world she lives in. Her daughter is a year older than Wil and has a bunch of diagnosis: cerebral palsy, autism, maybe an intellectual disability, too. Kerstin has therapists coming to her house all the time and doing what they call ABA, Applied Behavioral Analysis with Brooke. No, Kerstin is not being grumpy, she is being realistic. Now I am grumpy.

I call Dr. Willis anyway, even though there is a big what-am-I-getting-myself-into fear. Greater than that, is a knowing that he has not reached out to us by accident. We are being handed a gift, and it's our job to take it – however it comes wrapped.

We walk into Dr. Willis' office at Emanuel Children's Hospital. He sits in a green leather chair and asks us all the same questions that Dr. Budden and PeiP asked: pregnancy history, birth weight, and gestational time. I am already tired of these questions and I am just a couple months into them. Is this how it's going to be for the rest of my life? Whenever someone tries to help Wil are they are first going to blame me? Or at least try?

Sure enough, Dr. Willis tells us about Stanley Greenspan's groundbreaking work with Floor Time and gives us the quick and dirty explanation. He gets Ed, Wil and me all down on the floor and as he tells us how to engage Wil, he videotapes us.

"Don't just hand him the toys," Dr. Willis says, "give it a name and see if you can get him to make a sound of some kind, or at least reach for the toy and make some effort to communicate his desire for it."

"Wil," I say his name with a pause before continuing – just like a dog, giving him a moment to click in that I'm talking to him. "Wil...do you want to play with the train? Can you say, 'train?' Say, 'train.'"

Frustrating your child on purpose, even if two biggie doctors tell you it's all for the best, feels cruel to me.

We're carting him to Dr. Willis' every two weeks to sit on the floor and be taught how to pry communication out of him. In front of a camera. Then that video gets shown to a group of students Stanley Greenspan is coaching, and they pick us apart.

A couple months into the project Dr. Willis calls us to review the tape of the "experts" that have reviewed our tape. We are torn limb from limb.

"The mom uses educational-ese, but doesn't know what she's doing."

Darn right I use educational-ese. I have a Master's in education. What do these twenty-five-year-olds know about *anything?*

I want to yell and scream and have a good cry. We are nobody's guinea pigs, this was supposed to be helping Wil. Tearing me apart is not helping anyone, and thank you very much, but we are taking our child and leaving now. We don't need a panel of experts to tell us if that's okay or not.

But we didn't stay gone.

I speak up the next time we have an appointment. "While this process may be helpful to your students, it is not helpful to us. We wish to discontinue this project," I said to the bespectacled Dr. Willis. As I sit on my love seat, perpendicular to Ed's, my eyes catch something by the door. A crucifix. Dr. Willis is a man of faith. Not only that, he is Catholic. I hadn't known that about him and it shifts something inside of me. I shift in my seat and I shift my attitude. I know now that Dr. Willis is on our cosmic team.

As we leave the hospital and look for our car in the parking lot, I see my fairly new black Honda CR-V. When the license plate arrived, I tried to think of an acronym to help me remember the first three letters, VRJ. "Very Ruth and Jim" I decided, thinking of my mom and former stepfather. That didn't really even make sense, but on the rare occasions I had to recite my license plate number, I was able to. Today, I see those three letters differently, not as an acronym but as an abbreviation. VRJ – Virg, short for Virgin, as in Mary.

CHAPTER SIX

Wil is in an Early Intervention preschool two afternoons a week across town. If I wanted, a taxicab could come and get him at our house and take him to preschool, then bring him back home when it is over, two hours later. For the life of me I cannot imagine putting a non-verbal child alone in a car with a stranger and going about my merry way while God knows what is happening to him. Apparently I am the only one who feels this way. In Wil's class there are five other kids, none of them verbal, one not even ambulatory and they all arrive by cab. Maybe all the other parents are single or working or busy with other children at home.

There is a teacher, a speech pathologist, an occupational therapist and an aide named Mark. Not only am I the only parent that drives him here, I also stay for most of the class, as Wil is not happy when I'm not attached to him. Together we sing, "Ring Around the Rosie," and other preschool songs. We sit in tiny chairs around the snack table and are shown picture cards and asked to make approximate sounds indicating if we'd like Cheerios, Froot Loops or graham crackers for our snack. Next comes the juice. Wil does not like juice but is not able to articulate that yet. I show him the picture for water and gently move his pointer finger to it and say, "Water."

On the days he is less clingy, I leave him there and quickly run to the nearby Fred Meyer to do some grocery shopping all alone. I'm quickly reminded of our early days in the big, wide aisles of a different Fred Meyer on hot summer nights, and I realize that while we have not come far, we have arrived somewhere else. The crying has stopped for the most part. The brushing therapy really helped and all the other things we did to re-set his sensory system: joint compressions, wrapping him in blankets, swinging him like he was a hammock and getting his feet to walk on surfaces like concrete and grass.

In Wil's class there is a little girl named Iris. She has

cerebral palsy and cannot move any of her body on her own accord. Her mother is nineteen. She came one day and I got to meet her. She was a lovely girl. A girl, though, not a woman. This job is hard enough for me at thirty-three. Not a day goes by that I'm not grateful for being as old as I am, with as much education as I have, relative financial stability, and full family support. How do others less fortunate than I manage?

Mark is Wil's favorite. He is young himself, early twenties. He wears a wedding ring and mentions his wife, but it's hard to believe he's married. He seems like he's about fifteen. He gets down on the floor with the kids and plays. He chases them up the ladders and catches them as they come down the indoor, plastic slide. He sings and claps and cheers and praises. I love Mark.

"Crayons go on paper!" the speech path says in a sing-song voice every time a child writes on anything but.

"Feet on the floor!" she sings when a child attempts to climb up on anything other than the indoor play equipment.

"Chairs are for sitting!" we hear when someone uses one for a stepstool.

I like the emphasis on the positive and this room is full of people who love kids and it shows. Because I am in the room so much and none of the other parents are, they tend to forget I'm there and talk as though I'm not.

"That's just echolalia," the speech path says when the OT reports a child has said something interesting. I don't know what echolalia is, but they throw this around when one of the kids says something repetitious and meaningless. Echolalia, from the sounds of it, means fake language – what you might hear as you bellow inside a cold, dark cave, hoping that someone else is in there and only having your own voice bounce back to you for company.

We finish the year of preschool and the PeiP team meets with us to determine placement for next year.

"There is a classroom we think would be a really good fit

for Wil," they tell us. "It's in Northeast Portland – a bit of a drive, but Teacher Carol has done this forever and I know you'll just love her."

The minute we walk into Carol's bright, happy, well-organized classroom we are relieved. She's a late fifties pixie with high energy and a smile that would light Manhattan. We are in love.

Carol has a speech pathologist, an aide and five other students, including Cody, a boy with Down syndrome. I spend the first several weeks staying the whole time with Wil, but by November I am able to drop him off, go to the nearest coffee shop and get back in time to grab him, throw him in his car seat with Big Bird, his fafa and Goldfish, and buzz back to get Jane before she's out of kindergarten.

This is my first year of not working at all. I had to drop my one-day-a-week job teaching when Jane started kindergarten and Wil began all his therapies and two different schools. It had simply become too much for all of us and not making enough to afford different childcare, I stopped teaching altogether. I miss a lot of things about working away from home one day a week. I miss the social piece. I miss the brain engagement. I miss being good at something, because the fact of the matter is, nothing around here is pointing to the fact that I'm good at this.

CHAPTER SEVEN

A childhood friend of mine is getting married and there is a bridal shower. I get Ed to watch both kids and I spend a few extra minutes in front of the mirror trying to put some extra effort into my appearance, something I am just now starting to do. For the first three years of Wil's life, my attitude was *why bother?* But everyone says if you feel better about yourself, you'll feel better about everything else. So I brush my shoulder-length dirty blond hair and make a mental note to get an appointment with the hairdresser. A cut and some highlights would definitely help the situation. I put on silver hoop earrings, button up a freshly ironed white blouse and pull on black tights, a black corduroy skirt and some black boots. I feel almost sassy.

I kiss and say goodbye to Ed and the kids and nearly run out the door and jump in my car. Things aren't as bad as they were when Wil was first born, but they are still hard. I love Ed, and he loves me, that will never change, but there is just no time for each other. We don't discuss this, however, because A) there is no time, and B) there is no energy for such discussions, I think we both have the let's-just-get-through-this attitude. I've heard that having a special needs child either tears you apart or brings you closer together. I've also heard that eighty percent of couples with a special needs child get divorced. That may very well be true and I understand completely. On one level it would make so much more sense to live in two different houses, to spell each other, to have periods of being "off" and to recover. Respite.

Still, there is deep love, trust and commitment in our marriage. And by the grace of God, there is humor. Dark humor, silly humor, only-funny-to-us humor. Lots and lots of humor. We are all-hands-on-deck to intervene with Wil right now; triage. The bleeding is Wil, and until it stops -- and we

believe it will someday -- he is where all the attention must go.
I think about all this as I drive to the bridal shower on this
gorgeous fall evening with the moon shining brightly up in the
sky. Fall. A time of harvesting what you've planted. A time of
bringing in the crops and storing them for the winter – the
impending death and stillness. The seasons fascinate me and I
once had an astrologer try to explain them in terms of our life
cycles. From what she said, Ed and I are in the period of
spring in our marriage and in our childrearing. Everyone
thinks, *Oh, yea, spring, what a cheery time of year!* No. On the
contrary. Astrologically speaking, spring is the hardest season
to be in. It's a pushing-through time. It's the seedlings being
under the ground, cold and damp from the winter and in the
starting blocks. Tremendous effort is required to shove them
up and out of the warm, dark earth and expose them to the
light.

That's about right. Ed and I are indeed in the springtime of
our lives. Everywhere we look there is darkness and effort to
push through it to be where we have heard the light is – on the
other end of the interventions, when the kids are both older,
when we have gotten into our forties, when lots of other things
happen and change - but not now.

My friend who is getting married is Missy. Melissa is what
she prefers to be called now, but to me, she will always be
Missy. We have known each other our whole lives.

As a child, Missy's grandmother gave her a subscription to
Bride magazine. Missy and I would pour through those
magazines talking and planning our future weddings, then act
them with our Barbie and Ken dolls. It was settled. I would
marry a man named John and she would marry a man named
Jeff. We would be in each other's weddings and our dresses
would be spectacular.

Turns out by the time I actually did get married at almost
twenty-nine, I cared very little about a wedding and even less
about the dress. I wanted no part of a big to-do. No part of
getting both my not-on-speaking-terms parents under one roof
and no part of being the center of attention. Plus, the practical

side of me thought, *I'd much rather spend my money on a honeymoon.* Ed was thrilled when I suggested we do an announced elopement and come home and have a big party. Ed had proposed to me in April and by May I had moved in with him with a December wedding date on the calendar. I was teaching and the logical time to take off for a honeymoon was Christmas vacation.

We had a ball and I hope Jane does the exact same thing some day. I spent about an hour shopping for my perfectly fine wedding dress and Ed picked up matching flip-flops and a Hawaiian shirt the day before the big event. We had several days alone in paradise before the wedding. The wedding day itself was spent lounging by the pool and relaxing before finally driving our rental car out to the site on Kauai where "South Pacific" was filmed – at the site of the famous waterfall. The whole thing was cheesy, cheap, lovely and delightful in every way.

I couldn't wait to see what Missy would do for her wedding. Would she, too, radically change directions from what she'd always planned, or would she stick to tradition and childhood dreams?

I followed the directions I'd written down and found their house to be a cute 1920's bungalow near our old house in Northeast Portland. I parked, went in alone, and hoped to God I'd spot Missy right away. "Carrie!" I heard her shout before I was even in the door. Missy is about as big as a minute, just a little over five feet tall and can't weigh an ounce more than one hundred pounds. She has big brown eyes and brown hair with blond highlights. She is a runner now, just did a marathon she tells me. She introduces me to her friends and they are all super nice, stunningly beautiful and I am suddenly conscious of my out-of-fashion clothes that are the nicest things I own. I am thirty-six-years-old and feeling very middle aged.

Missy leaves me to attend to the other guests. One of her friends and I start chatting. "There is going to be a Tarot card reader here tonight, come here, I'll show you," says the model-beautiful-less-than-thirty-and-never-had-kids friend. She pulls me into the kitchen where instead of overhead lights there are candles lit all over and a lacey curtain covering the entrance to a built-in niche where the Tarot readings would be conducted. I start to freak out. *Oh, it's a good thing my Baptist- minister's-wife-grandmother will never know about this because if she weren't already dead, this would kill her.* I have come a long way in shedding the fundamentalist beliefs instilled in me by my mother and grandmother.

I was taught that all rock stars were devil worshippers and by rock stars I mean Barry Manilow and John Denver. I was forbidden to put up their posters, but I could listen to their music. My grandfather believed the devil hid in the corners of fitted sheets.

The devil also lived in playing cards and while Grandma and Grandpa were around we could never play Hearts, Gin Rummy or even Go Fish! Of course drinking, smoking and swearing were forbidden.

Tarot, Ouiji Boards, séances, all of that was work of the devil, and there was a big part of me that wanted to bolt as soon as I saw that lacey curtain and all those spooky candles. It's a good thing Missy failed to mention the Tarot card reader, or I never would have come in the first place.

I slip into the bathroom, close and lock the door and take a minute to gather myself. I remind myself that I can leave at any time; I have my own car and am a grown-up, for heaven's sake. I also remind myself that no one can make me have my cards read, that I can simply and politely decline. And yet, I believe there are no accidents. Maybe there is a bigger purpose to me being here than to simply celebrate Missy's impending wedding. Maybe right here is exactly where I'm supposed to be. Maybe the Tarot card reader has something to tell me that I need and am ready to hear.

We proceed through the shower, eating fancy food, drinking yummy wine and opening gifts while one-by-one each guest slips away to have her cards read. Finally, someone taps me on the shoulder and lets me know it's my turn. I walk to the kitchen, part the lace and sit down across from a woman with waist-length brown wavy hair and a very kind face. She looks to be about my age, but it's hard to tell. She looks like she's probably a vegan, does yoga and never drinks caffeine. Those types always look younger than they really are, unlike me, who must look at least ten years older than my actual age. "I'm Wendy," she says. "Don't be nervous." *Shoot!* I think, *she's a mind reader, too!* "Let's just start really slowly. Tell me your name, the spelling, and your birth date.

"Carrie, C-A-R-R-I-E. February 14, 1963."

Wendy does not say, "Oh! A Valentine!" as pretty much everyone else says when I tell them my birthday. I do not know how to interpret this and decide to chalk it up to her being professional. Wendy writes the information on a tiny notepad sitting beside her, stares at it for an awkward moment, then tells me to shuffle the cards any way I want, for as long as I want.

"I'm done," I say, handing the whole deck back to Wendy making it her problem again.

She turns cards over and makes an arrangement on the table. I see the picture of a man hanging upside down from a tree by one foot. On the bottom of the card it says, "Hanged Man" and my stomach drops. Hanged Man cannot be good, I'm thinking. Hanged Man must be very bad. Maybe I'm going to die. I would have been so much happier not knowing I was going to die. I would rather just, *bam*, drop dead than know I was going to die. What am I going to do with this new knowledge of my imminent death?

"We will go through this card-by-card," Wendy says. I see you looking at Hanged Man. Don't worry. The cards are not literal. I will explain everything.

I hear, "Blah, blah, blah" until finally, about the fifth card, she gets to Hanged Man. "See how Hanged Man is suspended by the tree by his foot, not his neck? This is not about life and death; it's a time of suspension. You are in a period of trial, a prolonged period of selflessness, sacrifice and indeed, prophecy. You will be best served by not resisting or opposing."

There are no accidents. Wendy's words drop deep. They comfort in a way that I had not expected.

I finish listening to Wendy as she tells me about the appearance of the Sun in my reading – a sign that all is going in the right direction. I know that she is right – my son is pointing me in the right direction. I know there is light to my story and his. I know that I will never forget her words and I will be tracking down her information and calling her again when I need spiritual direction. Grandma was wrong. Tarot is not the work of the devil. For the first time since Wil was born three years ago, I feel full of the Holy Spirit. Part of some plan. Part of something big. Part of something I don't even know what yet.

CHAPTER EIGHT

We moved two years ago from the teeny tiny house next door into this one. Now each kid has their own bedroom and there's much more room to spread out. Upstairs there are four bedrooms. The extra one is a play room where all the toys are as well as my desk and computer. At last, we aren't on top of each other and the stress level is much reduced.

No specialists come to the house anymore. Wil gets all his services through Peip's preschools. He is in Teacher Carol's afternoon class two days a week again this year plus goes three mornings a week to where Jane went to preschool, inside a local high school. With two teachers and at least fifteen high school age assistants, Wil should have the help he needs. Before the high school assistants can even take this class they have to have child development their freshman year and get their food handler's licenses. While Claudia is the official teacher, Sandra the assistant runs the show and is quick to laugh a big-hearted laugh. Everywhere you go in the very large spacious room, you can hear Sandra talking to one of the assistants or preschool kids.

"Justin, take Jacob over to the water table and see if you can get him to try that now!"

"Sarah, you and Natalie get started on the snacks!"

Sandra is bossy and loud, warm and wonderful. We adore her. When Jane did this program, I just dropped her off and came back, but most days I'm in here with Wil for at least twenty minutes. Then Sandra decided that it's best for Wil and me to change that up.

"Carrie, I have asked Ashley to be Wil's one-on-one aide. We don't normally do that because we like the high school students to be with all the kids and get as many different experiences as possible, but Ashley is one of our best, and I just think she'd be great for Wil. What do you think?"

I thought then and know now that Ashley is the answer to a multitude of prayers, both spoken and silent.

Here's our morning routine. We walk Jane to school and drop her off just a little after 8:00. We walk home and get straight in the car. We drive to Safeway, and whether we need a single thing or not, we go in. Wil calls it "Bye bye door," saying "door" for "store." Before we go in, I pin on the Safeway name badge that Marlies had made for Wil. "Wil" it simply says. Nobody needs to look at the badge. He is known by every employee who works that morning shift and there are many – including our old favorites - Marlies, Lonnie, Carmen, Carla, Steve and Larry.

On days Wil has morning preschool, we then drive to the high school. On the other days, and both Saturday and Sunday, we go home after going to Safeway. But we always go to Safeway. Always.

Wil runs down the aisles and I chase after him. Sometimes I have a cart and I madly throw things into it as I keep him from running into people, displays and other carts. Sometimes I have a little hand basket and toss in just a few little odds and ends. Often we just run through the aisles, shout goodbye to all our friends and run back out into the parking lot to find our car before heading off to preschool.

I have talked to Dr. Willis about Wil's running and the fact that he seems to have no awareness of danger. I can shout, "Wil! Stop! Car!" and he doesn't slow down for a minute. Dr. Willis is keeping his eye on him and thinks we may indeed be looking at ADHD.

"But aren't all little boys hyper?" I asked the first time he brought this up.

Dr. Willis replied, "The difference between Wil and a typical boy his age is that typical boys have periods of high activity and periods of rest. Wil just has high activity." I spend the next several months pondering that.

I look for periods of rest with Wil, but there aren't any. Even when he sleeps, he's all over the bed, noisy and busy. He stands to watch TV and can only watch a few minutes before becoming bored. He's more interested in changing the channels with the remote than in actually watching anything except "Yo, Five," and a tiny bit of "Sesame Street." There is also one little video he'll let me play with preschoolers singing Bible songs. He won't let me leave it on very long, but he tries to clap and dance and it's about the cutest thing you've ever seen when he does.

At school, both kids are practicing for their Christmas program. Jane's first grade class will sing songs of Jesus and not an eye will be dry. Wil's class, because it is in the public school system, will have a "winter program". They will sing songs about Hanukkah and Kwanza, and the Christmas ones will be all about Frosty and Rudolph. That's okay, I get it, that's the way it has to be, but it's a shame because Wil's favorite songs are all about God. We still play the "Wee Sing Bible Songs" tape in my car every time we drive. It's going to wear out and snap in half one of these days. I've tried other tapes and they simply won't do. "NO!" he shouts and so back we go to "Wee Sing Bible Songs".

I want the kids to see Santa. I want them to sit on his lap and tell them what they want for Christmas. I want to get a babysitter and go buy every single thing on their lists. I want to find special Santa wrapping paper, wrap those gifts in it and place them by their stockings that my mom made them with their names on them. I'll lay them lovingly by the fireplace next to the cookies we will make ourselves, a glass of milk and carrots for the reindeer. I want a perfect childhood for both of my kids, and Santa is a big part of that.

They talk about Santa all the time at preschool and Wil shows no interest or comprehension of what they're talking about. Every time one of his teachers or high school assistants, or even Ashley, asks, "Wil, what do you want Santa to bring you?" he runs off in a different direction without answering the question.

"Come on, kids, let's get dressed and go see Santa!" I say as I pull out a Christmas dress for six-year-old Jane, red tights and black Mary Jane's. I yank a red turtleneck over Wil's big three-year-old head and make him scream from the discomfort. He doesn't cry nearly as much as he used to, not like the days when he was absolutely inconsolable. Ever since we started the sensory integration therapy he's been so much better, but he still is a fussy kid and more often than not, I'm still holding him on one hip and jumping around.

Ed comes home early and we pile into the car to race to the mall. It's only the first week of December. We want to go see Santa before the crowds really get going. We've picked today, Monday, and this time, 4:00 PM, for that very reason. We should have Santa all to ourselves and that's the only way it can possibly work. If we time it just right we'll only stand in line five to ten minutes, we can throw Wil on one leg and Jane on the other, get a quick picture of the kids with Santa and call it good. Jane will tell Santa what she wants, and it will be modest and darling. She might say a Barbie or a game, but I know my girl and she'll only ask for one reasonable gift. If Wil holds off crying long enough to get the picture, I will be satisfied.

I get both kids on Santa's lap, snap a picture that is not bad, not great, just good enough. I have a feeling that "good enough" will become the theme of my mothering, my expectations and of my life.

It's Christmas morning. I have been up since 5:00. I want to make sure I have everything perfect before the kids wake up. I put cinnamon rolls into the oven. I made them late last night and they rose while we slept. Now they are huge and fat and will be delicious. Neither kid will touch them, but it's important to have the smell of cinnamon when they wake up and come down the stairs. I have coffee going, the lights on the tree are lit and there are a few other lamps on around the house to make it light enough to see where you're going, but not too bright to ruin the magic.

Wil wakes up first and we tell him he has to wait for Jane.

"Jay!" he calls, running into her room, flipping on the light and instantly waking her. At three he is just starting to talk and doesn't have a whole lot of words. It couldn't be any cuter how he made Jay out of Jane. We all call her that now, too. We'll probably call her that on her wedding day. It's just something she'll have to get used to and just one of the millions of ways her life is defined by being Wil's sister. She seems to have accepted that in a way only young children can.

We give Jane a minute to wake up and we change Wil's diaper — he is nowhere near ready to potty train. We make them wait at the top of the stairs while Ed and I dash downstairs to get the cameras. He shoots video and I click pictures.

"Let's see what Santa brought," I say as Jane runs to the fireplace and starts opening her stocking.

"Bye bye door!" Wil says, and begins to cry.

"Yes, honey, we will go to Safeway later. Right now it's Christmas morning! Time to see what Santa brought! Don't you want to open your presents?"

"Bye bye door!" he says again.

We try to ignore him as Jane finishes her gifts from Santa. Ed and I refill our coffee cups and move to more comfortable chairs around the tree. Wil continues to fuss and refuses to open even one gift. Jane is a good sport and Ed and I fake it through the whole thing. Finally, I can't stand it another minute.

"Okay, Wil. Let's get dressed and go to Safeway," I say. He stops fussing and lets me take him back upstairs to get dressed. We throw on clothes, grab my car keys, back out of the driveway and make the mile-and-a -half trip to Safeway.

Dark.

Closed.

"We will be closed on Christmas Day so that our employees may enjoy the day with their families," the sign on the door says. Certainly that sign has been there for at least a week. How could I not have seen it?

You don't see what you're not ready to see.

CHAPTER NINE

I hold my five-year-old son's hand and walk with trepidation into his Pre-K class. I thought for sure I would detect something different in the air today, but everyone seems to have signed a covenant to pretend nothing is wrong. Who are these people? Earlier this morning the sky fell. Literally. Fell in New York City and fell all over the world as terrorists attacked and we watched. Surreal.

My walking buddy Kathleen and I were up and out the door at 5:45 A.M. When I came back in the house, Ed was in front of the TV, "A plane crashed into the Twin Towers in New York."

"Accidentally?" I asked.

Before he could answer my question, we both stare at the TV and watch a second plane do the same thing. We don't know what to do, either of us, so we turn off the TV because we don't want the kids to see what we just saw.

I call the kids' schools to make sure they haven't cancelled school for the day, but they're open, business as usual. I can't get over how the teachers don't say a thing. Then again, what do I want them to do? Frighten the children? Tell a bunch of little kids their country is under attack? I don't have the answers, only questions.

This is Wil's first crack at being in a mainstream class with just a teacher and an aide — no specialists and nobody assigned just to him. Because he has a July birthday and is delayed both on paper and in life, we came to the decision that he needs a "bonus" year of preschool before starting kindergarten. I've searched all over, visited all kinds of preschools, talked to Dr. Willis, and the team from Peip, and found one that has pre-kindergarten for this very purpose; to help kids who need something between preschool and kindergarten.

For weeks I had been meeting with this teacher. I'd carefully gone over the facts of my son's special needs. I'd shared his IEP (Individualized Educational Plan) that qualified him for services with Portland Public Schools. I'd been very clear about his challenges, strengths and areas with which she'd need special help. We were set. They were ready for him. This woman had taught pre-school forever, there never had been a child she couldn't teach. She welcomed the challenge. I made the mistake of prematurely relaxing.

But on September 12, 2001, only a few days into the new school year, the teacher called me.

"Hi, Carrie, this is Michele, I'm afraid we are going to need to make other arrangements for Wil. This situation is not going to work after all. His needs are too great. I have called the directors of the school and there is room for him in a preschool class with fewer students, and where the pace is slower. He is spending all his time with the aide, Steve, and Steve can't help any of the other kids."

My first thought was not, *What am I going to do now?* but *Who dumps this on someone twenty-four hours after 9/11?*

CHAPTER TEN

We had been living in the house we built four years ago and there wasn't a thing wrong with it. It was on a very tiny lot, thirty-seven feet wide, but we had everything we could possibly need.

Then out of the blue, Ed comes home from a bike ride and says, "Care, you won't believe who just called me, the sisters!"

For the last five years Ed has been self-employed, working in our basement. He buys, sells, manages and develops real estate. For years, he's had his eye on a house in our neighborhood. "If we ever move, there's only one street I would move to. If we move to that street, there's only one block I would want. On that block, there is only one house I would want – it has an over-sized lot and we could add on." The house is owned by a holy order of nuns and is inhabited by two of them now. Every six months he's written a note to the headquarters, asking them to please let him know if they would ever consider selling it.

The woman that bequeathed the house to the nuns stipulated that it be used by the sisters for seven years. It had just reached the seven-year mark, so they were ready and willing to sell it.

"Make us an offer," they trustingly told Ed. When they accepted the offer, we went over to meet the nuns.

We walk up to the house, all four of us, and ring the doorbell. "Hi, I'm Sister Mary," she says. *Mary*, I think, *Of course your name is Mary. What else would it be?* I know the house is meant to be ours. It was just waiting and being blessed for us.

Sister Mary is about sixty-five but looks forty-five. I guess that's what never being married and having no children can do for you. She has an artistic looking cross around her neck – not a crucifix, I notice, and I like that about her immediately. I can see she is a contemporary nun.

She invites us in to see the house and explains that another nun - Sister Phyllis, lives there too, when not in Peru doing missionary work. Sister Mary's work takes place here in the house, which she calls the Hearth. People gather here several times each week for Tai Chi, Bible study, contemplative prayer and to study the works of Thomas Merton.

"I'm sad to be leaving," she confesses, "but most of the people who come here are getting older, including me. We really need to find something that's one story. It's the will of God that you have the house now. You will do important work here, too."

"I will find you the perfect one-story house," Ed assures her, as Sister Mary leads us through the house, past the 1950's kitchen, upstairs to the bedrooms and down into the paneled basement. There is very little about the house that I want to keep, every surface needs updating, but there is one thing I hope won't be removed during a remodel, and that is the undeniably good feel of the house. If houses have energy, and I believe they do, this one has the best of any I've ever been in before.

"Tell us about the house, Sister Mary," I ask.

"Let's all come sit down," she says and we follow her into the large living room. Once seated, she tells us. "In 1923, a little girl named Hortence and her parents built this house. She never married and after her parents died, she lived here alone until she was an old woman. She had two friends that worked at Safeway, where each morning she would go and have a visit." I couldn't believe I was hearing that the woman who left this house had visited Safeway – our Safeway, every morning.

Sister Mary continues, "One of Hortence's friends had a sister who was a nun for our order and who suggested Hortence leave the house to the order when she died. Hortence agreed and for reasons we never learned stipulated we were to do our work in the house for seven years before selling it. That's where you come in."

Wil is uncharacteristically quiet, allowing Sister Mary to tell the whole story without us having to get up and go chase him around somewhere, or ask him to please be quiet and not interrupt.

"We've taken up enough of your time, Sister Mary," I say while getting up. "Thank you for showing us the house and for being so gracious about something that must be so hard for you. We appreciate that."

"You're welcome, my dears," she says as she hugs us all goodbye. "When the house is empty and we've moved, but before you move in, we'll all meet back here and do a blessing. It's important to have rituals. The house needs to know that we are leaving and now it's yours."

"Sister Mary," I say, "we will continue to do good things in this house. We will open it up for events and gatherings that continue to do the important things you've started here. They will be different, but they will keep the good work and the love going," I assure her -- not knowing I was thinking that or going to say it until the words had already spilled out. Upon hearing them, however, I know they are true.

CHAPTER ELEVEN

I am about to turn thirty-nine. I don't feel freaked out about that, per se, but something is bothering me and I can't put my finger on it. I feel like I have a gun to my head at all times. Just standing at the kitchen sink washing dishes finds me in a panic. My chest feels tight. I sometimes start to sweat and occasionally my arms even get numb. Wil is noisy one hundred percent of the time. I can't believe we spent untold dollars and hours trying to get him to make utterances and now he does nothing but talk and move and repeat and generally drive me crazy. He is forever waiting for me and trying to hurry me up.

This year he is in kindergarten at Jane's school. It's a half-day program, and like Jane did, he goes in the afternoon. On Mondays, my mom is the helper. On Tuesdays, Ed's mom Doreen helps. Different parents fill in on the other days, including me. Because the "day" is only three hours long and there are only ten kids in the class and because there are always at least two adults in the room, it's working. On the days that I'm the parent helper in Wil's class, my favorite time of day is prayer time. The teacher has written a prayer that we all close our eyes and say together at the start of each class:

Lord, open our eyes to see beauty
Open our ears to hear truth
Open our minds to seek wisdom,
Open our mouths to speak kindness,
And open our hearts to love.
Amen.

The teacher really understands the needs and ways of young children, and if you ask me, she really understands prayer. I can hardly think of a more perfect one.

If Wil were to go to the neighborhood public school, he would be getting speech and language services, plus occupational therapy to help with his fine motor delays. However, the Catholic school doesn't provide those services. As such, he only gets thirty minutes a week of speech services for which I have to pick him up from his school, drive him to the neighborhood public school, sit there and wait for him in the hall outside, and then drive him back. It's ok, but it's not great. Truth be told, I can't see how what the speech pathologist has him doing is really all that different from what the kindergarten teacher is. Basically, the goal is to get him to expand his language, to ask for what he wants, be polite and to take turns.

People, especially my Catholic friends who went through parochial school, think I'm nuts for putting my kids there. Then they hear about Wil's needs and think I'm more than nuts. "It's not like it used to be," I say, which is true. Catholic schools are no longer run by tyrannical nuns. There is no corporal punishment, no guilt, no shame.

We know Wil's needs are beyond the scope of a traditional K-8 Catholic school, but the difference for us, is the faith-based community. We believe that Wil is of God first, and of man (and school), second. His ABCs and 123's are not nearly as important to us as his spiritual development and having him embraced, protected, nurtured and loved within a community. We found that in the Catholic school and that is where he is staying.

For his OT – occupational therapy - services we've found a great place in Portland that I take him to once a week for an hour. There are two rooms, one in which he wears headphones and hears a program that's supposed to regulate and organize the brain while the therapist plays board games with him. The other room is a huge gym with mats, ladders, swings and hammocks. Apparently a properly working vestibular system does more than provide balance. Kids with ADHD and Sensory Integration Disorder like Wil need help with this, and when they climb through, in and around this colorful obstacle course, it's supposed to help. Wil likes coming and that's enough for me. Any therapy he's getting in addition is just a bonus. He has a beautiful young therapist named Sarah.

Unlike speech therapy where Wil wants me to sit outside the classroom in which he's working with the door open and wait, I get to leave when he's at OT. During Wil's speech sessions I try to read a book while I wait outside the door, but the floor is cold, the school hallways noisy, and I'm totally distracted by how distracted Wil is while working with Shelley, the speech path. Shelley is kind and well-meaning, but Wil is not buying what she's selling. I can hardly think of anything but what a huge waste of time this is, as well as a giant pain.

At OT, once I've passed Wil to Sarah, I jump into my car and drive to the nearest coffee shop, where I order some seasonal latte and sit there with my book or computer or Suduko puzzle book and bliss out. And yet even in my happy hour, there is a sense of anxiousness I cannot shake. Some days, I forgo the latte and the noise of the coffee shop and instead, sit in my car and just breathe deeply. Some haphazard type of meditation. There is a deep conflict within me. I cannot use my time away from Wil to actually detach and recover from him. My mind is compulsive and obsessive and every thought path leads back to him.

There are days I can get myself hyperventilating thinking about the future. Even first grade is daunting. How is he going to get through school? Where will he go to school if we can't make this work? Will he be bullied? Will he be able to go to college? Will he be able to live alone, independently? Will I be parenting this hyperactive, loving, funny, exhausting, all-consuming boy for the rest of my life? And worse yet, what happens to him if something happens to me? Ed is a wonderful father and can do a lot, but he can't be a mother. This boy needs a mother.

The kindergarten teacher has been working with preschoolers and kindergarteners her whole career, which is a very long time. She is warm and generous, funny and kind, bossy and efficient. She is my kind of woman. We have formed a little friendship over the months Wil's been in her classroom, and she has already tipped me off to the fact that she thinks

Wil is going to need more help in first grade than he's getting now. In first grade, there aren't two small morning and afternoon classes. Instead, there is one big class of twenty-eight students. He will be lost. This is the root of my anxiety. Two years ago, I approached the school and discussed their need for a Resource Room: a place and program for kids with special needs. The school was on board and apparently the need had been recognized for years, but the money needed was always out of reach. Nonetheless, we formed a committee and I'd been working ever since to gather data, funding options and to gently but persistently push. A squeaky wheel. Squeak, squeak, squeak. I have learned from the best, Wil, and I will take this lesson and apply it to his future. So help me God.

> Lord, open my eyes to see beauty,
> Open my ears to hear truth,
> Open my mind to seek wisdom,
> Open my mouth to speak kindness
> And open my heart to love.
> Amen.

CHAPTER TWELVE

I am taking both kids over the mountain to Sisters to visit my mom. Ed is living one of his life-long dreams to go to the Daytona 500. The race happened to fall on my thirty-ninth birthday and he hesitated, but I insisted he go. He needs to get away and we will all have fun at my mom's.

"Go," I told him. "It's not my fortieth. I'll make sure you don't mess that one up."

It's mid-February and the Cascade Mountains are covered in snow. I have the back of my Honda loaded with chains, boots, rain gear and kitty litter to spread if I need to build traction. Ed and his dad even made me little wooden ramps to drive my front wheels up on, so I can hook those chains in the back of the tires. We are set.

Both kids are in the backseat. I picked them up from school at 3:15 and away we went. Jane is eight, in third grade and is an excellent traveler. She is content to sit with Fossie and Bear, the same ones she's been lugging around since she was a baby, and just stare out the window and let her mind wander. She reminds me of me in so many ways. I looked just like her at that age. Stringy dirty-blond hair, big blue eyes, skinny as a rail. She also has my personality in many ways, although she's a black and white thinker like Ed. We joke and say if Jane ever takes drugs as a teen, it'll be because she thinks it's a really good idea. Nobody can talk that girl into anything she doesn't want to do. She knows what she does and does not want, and self-advocates like nobody's business.

Wil, at six and in kindergarten still cannot begin to entertain himself. I have a million snacks in a bag right by me in the car and I just keep passing them back to him in an effort to keep him busy. I'll have to vacuum all the Goldfish and other crumbs up eventually, but right now it's worth it. I have a ton of books, too, but the only ones he likes are the big ones with noisy buttons along the side. The idea is to read the story and when you come to the symbol, you find it along the side and press it for effect. A car horn honking. A duck quacking. A bumblebee buzzing. Wil thrashes through the pages in no order whatsoever, and randomly presses the noisy buttons. He is prone to finding a sound he likes and pressing it repeatedly for ten or fifteen minutes. This is the kind of thing that would have made me stark raving mad before he was born, but I am learning to tune it out, now. The annoying sound is so much easier on the nerves than having him ask me a million questions, never listening to the answers. With Wil there are always two or more things happening at any given moment. Trying to focus on one and control his conversation is futile. But still I try.

We make it all the way over the mountain without having to stop and put on the chains, but as soon as I see the sign that says, "Carry chains or traction tires required," I feel myself tense up. Even though Ed and I have practiced putting on my chains in the warm, dry garage, the thought of actually doing it while both kids wait for me fills me with anxiety. Plus, the sign just bugs me. How practical would it be to carry traction tires? I'm sure they mean USE traction tires or carry chains, but that is not what the sign says and I spend way too much time agonizing about this each and every time I cross the mountain to see Mom, which over the years has been approximately a million times.

There is something about getting past the halfway point, Mill City, that starts to ease my mind every time. The scenery and trees change, the air smells different, the rain stops and turns to snow. I love the Willamette Valley, have lived there my whole life and plan to live the rest of my life there, too, but there is something instantly and deeply healing about crossing the Cascades and getting into the high desert of Central Oregon.

There is something going on with my legs, they feel unstable and even pushing on the gas pedal feels like exertion. My arms are a little tingly, too, and my chest feels tight. There's not pain, but if I wanted to take a deep, really deep, breath, it would be hard. This all diminishes as I pull into Mom's modest cul-de-sac and enter her three-bedroom, one-bath, little ranch-style house.

My mom is a former early childhood teacher. She loves kids and although she is glad to see me, it's all about the kids when we get there, which suits me just fine. I want to check out and try to relax, not be on full-alert duty.

After the kids are fed, bathed and in bed, I go to bed myself and try to read. Fifteen minutes into it, I turn off the light and close my eyes but I can't find sleep. My heart races. Now there is chest pain. There is some kind of Charlie horse thing going on with my left leg. My right arm is nearly numb. I think of asking Mom to take me to the ER, but I don't want to load up the kids and drive all the way into Bend, at least thirty minutes away. The more I debate whether or not I need to be seen by the doctor, the worse my symptoms get. I fight with myself all night, barely sleeping, finally deciding if I don't feel any better in the morning, I will ask to see Mom's doctor here in town.

The next day I do not feel any better, I feel worse. I decide going on a walk alone is just the ticket. I am forced to stop several times on the three-mile walk to catch my breath. A walk that I've completed easily for years is daunting today. I can't catch my breath. My head is pounding with pain. My arms are both numb now. I am sweating despite the below freezing temperatures. I wrestle all the way back to Mom's about what to do and again, decide not to do anything.

Finally, it's Sunday and time to go back to Portland. I feel even worse. All the way over the mountains there is snow falling. I can barely see the road ahead of me. I don't need to put on chains, however, because the snowplow has just been through and there is fresh sand all over the highway. On a windy, snowy, shoulder-less road my heart starts to pound so loudly I can hear it. I am sure I'm having a heart attack. I rationalize in my head that there's nothing I can do about it now. I pray that when I die, I will not kill anyone else or my children. I pray that someone will find the little "In Case of Emergency" list in my wallet and call Ed. I pray that he will somehow get from Daytona, Florida to Central Oregon to identify the body and care for his now motherless children. All of this makes perfect sense to me and this nothing-I-can-do-about-it-now attitude brings a sick calm.

I drive for miles in this state, completely blocking Wil's requests for more Goldfish, Cheerios, water or books. I am in a zone. Once safely over the mountain, I consider pulling into the ER at the nearest hospital in Salem. I drive right by the exit, deciding I wouldn't know what to do with the kids as I was treated. I drive the remaining hour of the trip in a haze and then without even consciously deciding to, I drive straight to Ed's parents' house. I have not called them to let them know we are coming. I have no real plan once we get there. I ring their doorbell, Doreen answers, takes one look at me and asks, "What's wrong?"

"I'm having chest pains," I say.

"Don? Watch the kids," she says as she grabs her coat and purse. Don, at seventy-seven, has never once watched the kids without the help of Doreen. I don't care. I am so glad to have another living soul take over, I start to feel better immediately. Doreen drives me to the nearby hospital only a couple miles from their house. It's Sunday afternoon and the place is quiet. "She's having chest pains!" my usually modest, quiet, demure mother-in-law shouts as we enter the ER.

I am taken back and placed on a stretcher. They put a cuff on my arm. "Your blood pressure is extremely high," the nurse says. For some reason, this calms me. There is something about finally being in the ER with people who know what to do that brings me peace. Another nurse wheels over an EKG machine and attaches it to me. "You did not have, nor are you now having, a heart attack," the second nurse says. Relief floods me and I notice my arms no longer feel numb. My headache is excruciating, but nowhere else is there pain in my body. My legs feel fine again. My chest is not tight. I am exhausted and want to sleep for days. Except for my pounding head, I feel fine.

A doctor comes back to see me about an hour later. "What

happened?" I ask him.

"You had a panic attack," he says. "You are fine and can go home as soon as you feel ready, but I want you to go see your primary care physician on Monday. Your blood pressure was very high. We've got it down now, but it's still too high for someone your age. You need to get that checked out."

Doreen patiently waits for me to tell her I'm ready and reluctantly I do so. There is a part of me, a big part, that would like to live here forever, where other people take care of my children. Where qualified professionals take care of me and the world does not exist beyond this little curtained off room.

"Come back to the house and get your car," Doreen says, "then drive yourself home, make yourself a cup of tea and get in bed. Don and I will bring the kids over in a few hours. Just rest."

I go home, put on pajamas and climb into bed, skipping the tea. I then begin to cry and there is a worry I may never stop. All the things I could be doing with this rare time alone in my own house fight for brain space with the dire need for rest.

I rest.

I'm back at Dr. Miller's office, but this time it's about me. It took a panic attack and a trip to the ER -- my first ever -- to get my attention, but I have a job to do and can't do it without some help. I've asked some friends and done some research. I need Paxil. I have generalized anxiety disorder – I even took an online self-assessment and pretty much got one hundred percent.

Dr. Miller walks in, sees me up on the exam table and starts to chitchat. I cut him off, "I need Paxil," I say to him. He smiles a bit bemusedly. "Oh? You do? Tell me about that." I tell him about my one hundred percent on the online test. I tell him about my panic attack. He looks over the notes the hospital sent over, smiles in a way I find annoying, although these days I find everything annoying, and says, "Well, that is just the classic profile for people with generalized anxiety." He writes me a prescription for Paxil.

I take Paxil for six years and do not shed a single tear in that time.

CHAPTER THIRTEEN

Wil has pretty much learned to read by putting Closed Captioning on all our TVs and reading while the people on TV are talking. Brilliant. There is a downside, however, and that is his propensity for junk TV. A couple times he's been too quiet and I go in to see what he's watching and it's "The Maury Povich Show." He loves when they are doing one of their "You are not the father!" episodes. I hardly have the stomach for it, but from what I can gather, a woman who is either pregnant or has a child, has a couple men on the set at the same time. I think Maury's producers have done some DNA testing and they alone hold the secret as to who is actually the father of the child. There is build up and suspense, lots of whooping and hollering from the audience and then Maury, dragging it out, first letting the woman do some yelling and then the man or men, denying and yelling back, sometimes involving in-laws and friends, lets it almost come to blows. Finally, he then pulls a card from a sealed manila envelope and says, "_____, you are *not* the father," or in some cases, "_____, you *are* the father!" No matter what the response, at least half the people on the stage are jumping up and down happy or angry, yelling or swearing, cheering or raging while the audience is going crazy.

If that doesn't tell you all that's wrong with America and television, I don't know what does. Nonetheless, Wil finds it highly entertaining.

Lining up several of his "friends," a stuffed cat, Tom, Elmo, a bear named Lucky and Curious George, he grabs a small book by Jack Kornfield, *Buddha's Little Instruction Book* from the basket in the prayer room. He calls us all out to the front porch and seats us in the white double rocker or in one of the two metal rocking chairs that face our heavily walked street. "Mom! You hold Tom, Jane you hold Elmo, Daddy you hold Lucky and CG – Curious George!"

He's Maury and he builds the audience's energy like a pro, he paces back and forth. "George, do you think you're the father? Why? Daddy, make George tell us if he thinks he's the father."

Good naturedly, Ed holds Curious George up in front of his mouth and says, "I am *not* the father!"

Jane and I play along too, and I pretty much always say that yes, I think I am the father. That is the answer Wil is going for. He can't understand why everyone doesn't want to be a father, when clearly that's the highest calling there is. He tells me almost every day that he can't wait to have kids. "Mom, I will have five boys, just like Hal and Lois on 'Malcolm in the Middle.' You will live with us and you will help me with the five boys. My wife is going to work and my work is going to be to take care of the kids. You will help me. You will help me take care of my five kids, my five boys, like Hal and Lois. You will live with us and help me take care of my five boys."

Finally, "Maury" flips open randomly to a page of Buddhist wisdom and goes through the lineup. "Tom, you are *not* the father!" I am supposed to clap and yell and be happy even though two minutes ago I swore that yes, I thought I was the father. "Elmo, you are *not* the father!" Jane makes the compulsory whoops and whistles and then he slows the pace, walking between Lucky and George dramatically. "Lucky, you *are* the father! You *are* the father, Lucky! You *are* the father!" Ed claps and jumps up and down and acts as excited as one should act in such a situation.

"Lucky! You are the father! Are you just so excited, Lucky? You *are* the father!" Ed assures Wil that he is thrilled to be the father.

I think I saw something in Ed almost twenty years ago when I met him, something that let me know he'd be a great father. I don't think it was something he ever said or did, as much as it was a feeling, a knowing. Perhaps it was spending time around Ed's parents that made me come to this conclusion. Perhaps it was wishful thinking or it was simply that his name was Ed and my singular experience with a father figure named Ed – a favorite uncle - was powerful. I just know that at the moment Ed was holding up "Lucky" the bear -- he felt lucky. He felt lucky to be a father. He felt lucky to be Wil's father. He felt lucky to have the time and lack of pride that gives a man the freedom to sit on his front porch with half the neighborhood walking by at any given time, hold a stuffed animal on his lap, and proudly shout, "I *am* the father!"

CHAPTER FOURTEEN

Wil has gained less than five pounds in five years. He is not skinny, he is emaciated. We have been taking "drug holidays" – a break from his meds that have the side effect of an appetite suppressant - so that he'll eat more and we hope, gain some weight. He does indeed eat more, but then he just poops more, and since he will only poop in a Pull-Up, I am spending the day chasing a hyperactive, almost ten-year-old and wiping lots of poop off his bum.

One thing his meds help him with is impulse control. He has zero. This was actually why we put him on meds in the first place, at age four. The doctor told us he was very likely to run in front of a moving car and be killed. We knew he was right. Non-medicated he is still likely to run in front of a moving car, except I child lock all the doors when he's off meds now.

I took him to Safeway and Trader Joe's today - he was almost run down by a grocery cart at least ten times. He has no sense of other people's personal space, no sense of what may be around a corner, no sense of stranger danger.

He spoke to each and every person at both stores. I know for some, he made their day. He grabbed the barbeque chips at Trader Joe's as soon as they were scanned, kissed the bag passionately and exclaimed, "Oh, chips, you are like a son to me." He is particularly good at noticing the people nobody else notices. The obese, the infirm, the elderly, these are his favorites. It was darling when he actually was a toddler, now he isn't, and I still need to interpret everything he says to people. I still need to hold his hand, and still need to read others for signs that they want him to shut up. He cannot read these signs for himself and they do not understand. Even those who are amused are left puzzled.

Sometimes, I wish he had "something" that was easily recognizable like Down syndrome. There is no neat and tidy way to sum up Wil, other than he is one of a kind. Even in his world of special educators I am always told, "I've never had a kid like Wil before." Uniqueness is great, to a point, and then it becomes an albatross.

Finally home, exhausted from the heightened security and human sensitivities, I told him to go watch a show so I could unload the groceries and put them away. In the time it took me to do just that, ten minutes, fifteen max, he had managed to uncap every cap in the house. We now have glue sticks, Chapstick, and some nasty smelling Icy Hot oozing all over the carpets. He opened an entire box of Band-Aids, their sticky backs scattered everywhere. He found the paper cutter and shredded all the important papers on my desk, then grabbed the adjacent scissors and gave himself a haircut. He drained the new (huge) liquid Tide by opening the spout and walking away. He decided to make his own special blend of cinnamon sugar, leaving grit on every surface in the kitchen. He can't help it. He cannot control his impulses. It is all I can do to control mine.

It is starting to sink in, really sink in, that his delays are not really delays. Sure, there are some things he will eventually do, like poop in the toilet, I pray to God, but there is a whole host of things no amount of catching up is going to make him able to do. He will never drive a car, be in a relationship with the opposite sex, let alone marry. And here's the one that kills me when I let myself think about it, Wil will never be a parent.

Although it's probably been obvious to all his teachers and therapists, doctors and extended family members, it's something I am just now starting to face.

Yes, he would be a great father in so many ways; he would be loving and patient, careful and attentive, fun and playful. It's doubtful he will ever be able to hold a job that pays anything above minimum wage. He will not be able to pay bills, prepare meals, use a stove or oven, or manage a calendar. When I think how it takes both Ed and me and all of our education and variety of acquired skills along the way just to pull it off, I know in my heart of aching hearts that this is not something that's in the cards for Wil.

We went from seeing Dr. Willis every couple weeks to once

a month, and now we're down to every three months. The last time we sat on the green leather couches I said, "He'll be able to go to college, right?" I meant it. He looked at me kindly and said, "There is probably a different path for Wil." Of course in my gut I knew that, too. How can a boy who in fourth grade is barely reading, and needs a one-on-one aide for most everything, be on the college track? All his work is modified. Instead of doing twenty spelling words, he does ten. Instead of writing a forty-page state report, drawing maps and making citations, he is coming up with Fun Facts about Oregon.

It's hard not to worry about the future, it would be great to look into a crystal ball and see, really see that he will be fine. I worry incessantly about what will happen to him when Ed and I aren't around anymore, or are too old to take care of him. We are going to see a lawyer and make up a will. I don't want the burden to fall to Jane, but no matter how we provide for him, she will have a responsibility that no sibling deserves.

So obsessed am I with knowing that Wil will be okay, I do some research and find the name of a good clairvoyant. I have seen Wendy the Tarot card reader, several times through the years and I love her, but she's no longer reading cards. She finished her Doctorate degree and is a clinical psychologist now with a full practice.

I drive to a bookstore near our old house in Northeast Portland and find a place to park right in front. It's funny how when I search for the supernatural, it keeps bringing me back to the place where Wil was conceived ten years ago, the very same neighborhood, in fact. I tell the woman standing at the counter that I'm here to see Susan, and she tells me to have a look around and Susan will be with me shortly.

There are Tibetan prayer flags, singing bowls, malas, prayer wheels and incense; all things I recognize. Beautiful instrumental music plays from the speakers overhead and I relax a little, waiting for Susan to come and get me. Having worked with Wendy over the years, I'm not as nervous as I once would be, but I am still apprehensive as to what she will tell me about Wil, which is why I am here.

"Carrie, I'm Susan," a woman about my age and size says, extending her hand. She is blond, has a sturdy, Midwestern look, and is wearing natural fibers and clogs. "Please follow me," she says as she leads me to the back of the store and into a little room with a pocket door. "Tea?" she offers.

"No, thank you, I'm fine," I say, settling into my seat opposite from her at the little table. I get out my pad of paper and pen from my purse and am ready to get started.

Susan sits there smiling and looking slightly above my head for an awkward couple of minutes. I let my eyes wander around the tiny room and notice above us is a skylight with a beautiful blue fabric draped across it. The effect is sun and sky. There are paintings on the wall of angels and other celestial beings. There are other things on trays and tables behind and around Susan, things I don't recognize but find comfort in.

I've gotten a little lost in my thoughts and am startled when Susan suddenly laughs. "Oh, they are so funny! You have many guides and angels, Carrie. You are literally surrounded. I have been listening to them and they want me to tell you about your son. Was there another reason why you came here today, or would it be okay for me to tell you what they have to say?"

Tears spring to my eyes. I am both relieved and surprised that my angels and guides already know the deal with Wil. I wish I were a more spiritual person. I feel like I am *pretty* spiritual, but there is so much I still fear and try to control. I am suddenly filled with a sense of *there's no turning back now*. I have a deep knowing that whatever Susan is about to say will change the way I think about Wil, and me, and us, and our life together, forever.

"Please go ahead," I say.

"Carrie," she says, moving her eyes from above my head to straight into mine. "You have a divine son. He has the soul of the Dalai Lama. He is pure love. He has no ego."

Susan stops, looks at me for a second to see if she should go on. I give a quick nod and she continues, "You and Wil have a Mary/Jesus relationship. You have been called to bring forth a special son who is here to help and heal the world. He has a strong message and he needs your help to convey it. He is not broken, there is nothing wrong with him. He is perfect, but the world needs your help to see that. So many will see what he lacks and see him as broken and in need of fixing. He is not broken, he is open. What are considered disabilities by some are in fact, special abilities: abilities to see the God in everyone, to love without conditions, to be completely nonjudgmental. He has not lost his direct connection to God that all kids are born with but most lose by three or four. He remembers heaven. He remembers being in the holy presence of God and he will share his memories with you, but you will have to listen."

I leave Susan's little room after an hour, get back into my car, silence the radio and pray a prayer of thanksgiving all the way back home – to Wil.

"Goodnight, Wil," I say as I tuck him into bed. "Sleep tight. I love you. I'll see you in the morning."

"No, you'll see me at 9:52, remember?"

"Oh, yes, 9:52, see you then."

"Don't forget, OK?"

"OK," I assure.

Each night we have this same conversation with only the time I am to wake him changing occasionally. Nonetheless, each night he has big plans for when I wake him up. He will play basketball at the neighborhood school by himself. He will get to be the boss of me and he will get to play on my computer; all things forbidden during his normal waking hours.

Somehow each night I "forget," and each morning he berates me before beginning the whole routine again.

"Tonight wake me up at 9:52. OK? Don't forget. OK? Promise not to forget, OK?"

We have this conversation approximately two million times between the time he wakes up every morning and the time he goes to sleep.

"Mom, can I have an Otter Pop while I watch TV on your

bed?"

"No."

"Can I have an Otter Pop while I watch TV on your bed at 9:52 tonight when you wake me up?"

"Yes."

"THANK YOU! You are the best mom! I love you! You let me have Otter Pops at 9:52 on your bed! Oh, thank you, thank you, thank you. Now don't forget, OK?"

"OK."

"Mom, will you please stop being so bossy?"

"No. I am the mom. My job is to be the boss."

"Will you please stop being so bossy at 9:52?"

"Yes."

"THANK YOU! You are the best mom...."

And that's just the thing about Wil. He is on one hand exhausting, depleting, even infuriating, and on the other hand, he is delightful, loving, and infuses me with a spirit I didn't know was possible. If he were all one and not the other I would not appreciate his gifts, I don't think. I'd take them for granted just like I take for granted all the other abundant gifts in my life, but because he can go from crazy-making to energy-giving again and again and again, I'm left in a state of wonder and perhaps something that even touches joy.

Wil just came into my office to see what I was doing. He came with his smile and a song. His song, "We're Suffering," is one of our favorites. We don't like to suffer, but we love the suffering song.

I was working with Wil and another "special" friend of his at school, Jack, trying to make math facts more fun. Every time they got one right, we'd "high five" and I'd say, "Oh, yea, who's on fire?" Like with everything, I beat that dead horse silly, until finally Jack said, "Can I not be on fire anymore?"

"Sure, Sweetie, you don't have to be on fire, but how come?"

"Because I don't like to suffer!"

Realizing too late the literal thinking both these boys had, I apologized for suggesting we celebrate their suffering. They both forgave me and suggested we just switch the chant to, "We're suffering," instead of "Who's on fire?" We decided to "go big" with that. We stood, invented hip movements, a whole snapping of the fingers component and a bit of a head swirl. Suffering never looked so good.

A few days later, I got an e-mail from Jack's mom, Patty. "Today my son wanted to walk to school with his friends, without me. It was very, and I know you know, very hard for me to let go. I wanted to hold his hand walking to school like always. BUT, I still have my little first grader so off I let him go. Actually, he was behind us. So of course that drove me nuts because I could not see him. My daughter and I walked to school. Had time to do a loop because we were too early (I walk fast when I am nervous), and made our second turn around the block when I saw my son and his friends. Wil had joined the group. My son and Wil were holding hands."

For all the things Wil cannot do, and for all the diagnosed disabilities he has, he is at least as well-gifted in the sensitivity department. He thought nothing of grabbing an eleven-year-old boy's hand and walking down the street. Because the boy needed him to. Because the boy's mom needed him to. Because the universe needed him to.

"MOM! It is 7:14! I am going to poop at 7:15! Don't forget! Wake me up at 7:15! I will be hiding under my bed, so look for me there at 7:15! Don't forget!"

The next fifteen minutes we have a running monologue about what time it is. His watch is "funky," he thought it was waterproof, but ah, guess not. Could I fix it? Could I find his other two watches from wherever they are in the house? Could I find his small "clock" (calculator), 'cause he really needs to play basketball, "don't forget." How many baby wipes are in that newly opened package? Eighty? He wants to "smell." "Smells like eighty-two," he argues. Legs swing from the breakfast bar, bang, bang, banging into the counter. The time is announced every two seconds in a voice he's borrowed from Lois of Malcolm in the Middle. Toast is being made per his request; he wants "six," so the two I've made are each tri-cut. Not enough garlic salt, try again, oh, now too much, start over. Now he wants water with ice, five pieces of ice. "Did anyone drink from this already?" he asks about the cup I've just pulled from the cupboard. Oops, gotta jump off the bar stool and close the bathroom door. The bathroom doors must be closed at all times, don't you know? The pantry doors must be open at all times. When will I remember? What time is it on my watch? Same time as on your watch. Show me, don't forget....

Ding-dong, we both run to the door, he with his greasy toast hands locks the unlocked door, thus blocking my way to open it for the phone repair guy. Phone repair guy doesn't find any problem with our line, must be the phone.

Ring, ring, ring, phone that hasn't been working starts to work just to prove me wrong, Wil asks me who is calling while I am fifteen feet from the pre-answered phone. "I don't know," I answer. "But who is *calling*?" he re-asks, exasperated with me.

Jane is awake and wants two eggs "really" scrambled. She has re-takes today. She's not happy. Why did they lose her pictures the first time? Those were cute. Now she has a cold and her nose must have grown overnight because today it is huge and her picture will look ugly and everyone will see it in the yearbook and it's not even her fault because someone else is so stupid they lost her first set.

Ed wants to talk about a business deal he's been working on for years. Wants to re-hash it. Wants to go through the entire thing, from the top, again. Now, please.

Internet is not working. Comcast says it is. Computers say it isn't. Could I please figure that out so he can check his e-mail?

Ding-dong, phone guy is back, Wil re-locks the unlocked door again, more butter and crumbs covering the doorknob.

"Mom! I'm skating!"

"Yea, you're skating. Take the hat off your feet and put

your shoes on, please."

"But Mom! I'm skating!"

"MOM! I am going to look ugly for my re-takes!"

"Care! The Internet is still not working!"

Ring, ring, broken phone rings perfectly, phone man doesn't understand it.

"MOM!" Wil bellows in his Lois voice, "Can we have prayer time today, just you and me?"

"OK," I answer, praying he forgets.

"RIGHT NOW!"

"FINE!" I answer, irreverently.

We sit down at the prayer table (others call it a dining room table, but we don't dine, we pray). Each prayer time starts with drawing from a small velvet bag, the angel word-of-the-day. Wil is so squirrelly, he is still talking about Eastern time and asking if 2002 was five years ago?

"Yes, 2002 was five years ago, when you were five turning six, now you are ten turning eleven."

"Do you want to do prayer?" I ask, "or do you want to talk about numbers?"

"PRAYER!" he answers in the Lois voice.

"Let's try again, then. Pick a word."

Still with the numbers, times, dates, I lose it.

"I'LL DO PRAYER WITH YOU WHEN YOUR PATCH KICKS IN!" I shout, referring to the medicated patch he wears for his ADHD. It takes a long two hours to begin working, but when it does, it does.

Meanwhile, Ed is off in another part of the house trying to prepare himself mentally for his day. Yesterday at prayer time we read in *Warriors of the Light* that if you cannot quiet the mind enough to meditate, just repeat one word over and over again, until that word becomes your meditation.

Ed is in his chair, eyes closed, "love, love, love, love," he is quietly repeating, trying to find his groove and get into the now.

Wil, still at the prayer table, finds his favorite angel word-of-the-day, walks into the room where his daddy is, lifts up

Daddy's shirt, places the word on his chest, and says, "Here you go. Let this kick in," as if it were a medicated patch like he wears each day.

The word? Wil's favorite? The one he draws "randomly" day, after day, after day, no matter where we try to hide it in the stack of fifty? "Love."

Wil then turns to me and asks, "Mom, you know what the good thing about you is?"

"Tell me."

"You put me to prayer and live in my heart."

"Not yet, not yet!" he yells as I see his jammied body whiz by on the way from his bedroom to the bathroom. I am trying to write in the room right next to his. A look at my computer screen it tells me it's 6:15 AM. I take my first deep, cleansing breath of the day.

The lid of the toilet bangs, indicating it is up, and so is he. Another day has begun, officially.

The toilet lid bangs back down, he flushes, jabs his fingers under the running water to pacify me then runs the four feet back to his bedroom grabbing the blue and red car-shaped pillow off his bed.

"There," he says as the pillow lands on the floor next to my writing desk. "Now you can wake me up! You cannot wake me up until I pee. I have peed, so now you can wake me up! Come and wake me up, Mom! Come and wake me up!"

I pick up the car pillow, take another big breath, and walk next door to his room.

"WHO IS AWAKE IN HERE? WHO IS AWAKE IN HERE?" I bellow.

The red, white and blue of his quilt, covers the mound that is him. Fake snores come from the wiggling mass. I crawl next to him on the bottom bunk, lift the quilt from his face, and cover my nose and mouth with both hands.

"The breath! The breath! Not the breath!"

"Haaaaaaaaa" he exaggeratedly exhales.

"The breath! You're killing me with the breath!" This time I pretend to gag.

Eyes crusty with allergies, sandy blond hair poking up from the crew cut pushed askew from all the positions his body has been in on the bed since 8:30 last night, he sneezes twice, wiping his nose and eyes along the blue sleeve of his pajama top, leaving a white, shiny trail behind.

"Zero, blast off, one more time!" he informs me.

I put the bad breath joke through its paces until after "one more time" I lie writhing next to him, having all but died from the halitosis. He laughs so hard there is no sound. He cannot recover from laughing long enough to draw air.

"OK, OK! I am awake! Watch me get ready! Watch me put on my socks! Watch me go downstairs! Mom! Are you watching me? Don't forget to keep watching me!"

To the stairs we go, he with the NBA pajamas, size eight on his nearly eleven-year-old body, the waistband still too loose and landing south of its designated part of the body.

I have on any combination of pajama bottoms and T-shirt. Different mornings, different combinations, but all mornings blur into one. My love mug in my right hand accompanies me through the rigors of our routine.

"Wait! I need to bring Sam! Sam? Where are you, Sam? Are you awake, Sam? It is time to go downstairs and have breakfast, Sam!"

Having found the pink Build-A-Bear named Sam he is ready for the next phase of the morning routine.

"Stand behind me on the stairs, Mom. Do not go ahead of me. Wait for me, Mom. I will go down and you will follow me on the stairs. Do not go ahead of me, Mom. Wait for me."

He sits at the top of the stairs.

"You stand on that stair, Mom. I will go down and you will go down, but you cannot go down until I go down, OK, Mom? You will wait for me to go down, OK?"

As we descend the twelve wooden stairs together, he on his bottom, scooting down excruciatingly slowly, me impatiently standing behind him, he continues with the routine.

"Is your body awake yet, Mom?"

"Not yet, Love, not yet. My body is not all the way awake yet."

"But you have your coffee! Why is your body not awake if you have your coffee?"

"The coffee hasn't kicked in yet, Love."

"When will your body be awake Mom? Will it be awake at 6:30 AM PST? Will it be awake at 9:45 AM EST? What time will your body be awake?

"It will be awake at 7:55 AM"

"But that is when I will go to school, Mom! How come your body will wake up after I go to school? Will your body wake up before I go to school? I want your body to wake up before I go to school! I want your body to wake up at 10:00 AM EST. Promise your body will wake up at 10:00 AM EST? "

"OK, I promise."

Finally having reached the main floor, we walk together into the kitchen.

"Yea, Mom! Who is the best mom? I am so happy your body will be awake at 10:00 AM EST. Thank you for following directions, Mom! You are good at following directions, Mom! I am going to give you a star. Can I give you a star, Mom?"

Already standing before the art supplies, both cupboards flung open with a thud, knobs dinging the adjacent doors, paper pulled from the bottom of the stack, at least twenty extra pieces other than the one intended landing on the floor, he grabs a red one, his favorite color.

The nine-and-a-half by eleven inch piece of paper is soon filled with a single "A+." The A more of an upside down V, the crossing horizontal line so high and so tiny, it hardly constitutes an A. The + sign larger than the A. There is no more room on the paper for any more commentary. His hands have done their best to indicate what his brain is telling them. This is his best.

After he goes to school, after I clean up the kitchen, after I eat my breakfast and am finally ready to go back upstairs and finish whatever it was I was working on with my computer, I see that he's been there. I am at once grumpy. He is not allowed on my computer. Period. He's ruined three. Somehow he's figured out how to send me an e-mail from my computer to my computer. "I LOVE YOU MOM AT 7:00 EST TOMORROW." He's spelled tomorrow correctly. He has punctuation. He already has plans to love me tomorrow. He's just gained full access to computer number four.

"I am going to get Bart when I am one-one, Mom. On Saturday, July 14th at 12:00 midnight, I am going to get Bart, Mom. Did you know that? Did you know I am going to get Bart when I am one-one, Mom?"

"That's right, Wil, you are going to get your Bart Simpson toy on your birthday, when you are one-one: eleven."

"Are you excited for me to get my Bart, Mom? Are you excited that when I am one-one I will get Bart for my birthday, Mom? Aren't you happy, Mom?"

"I am super happy, Wil, I am super, super happy," I say, smiling, and meaning it.

We have a similar conversation approximately every two hours, for days, "Mom, I have a great idea! Let's go to Toys R Us at 11:59 PM tonight and get my Bart Simpson! Promise you will wake me up at 11:59 PM tonight and we will go to Toys R Us, Mom?"

"Sure," I answer.

"Promise you won't forget to wake me up at 11:59 tonight so we can go to Toys R Us, Mom. OK? Promise you won't forget?"

"I promise," I say, lying through my teeth.

Each morning I hear, "Mom! You did not wake me up at 11:59 last night! Why did you not wake me up at 11:59 last night, Mom? You were supposed to wake me up at 11:59 last night and take me to Toys R Us to get Bart Simpson! Why did you forget to wake me up last night, Mom? Wake me up tonight, and do not forget!"

I muster an unconvincing nod every ten minutes.

Finally, the day of his birthday arrives. Today is July 14th, my tall, crew-cutted blond, skinny, darling of a boy is eleven, or "one-one," as he prefers to be called. Wil says to me, "Mom! I have a great idea! We will just go to Toys R Us right now and get my Bart Simpson! Isn't that a great idea, Mom? Can't you believe what a great idea that is, Mom? We will just go right now to Toys R Us! We don't have to wait until 12:00! We can just go right now!"

I'd like to say, "I can't believe it's been eleven years since the day he was born," but I can believe it. So can my gray hair, lined face, high blood pressure and caffeine addicted body. I can believe it. What I can't believe, is that it hasn't been longer. I must be a hundred, maybe more. It's only 7:34 AM, 10:34 EDT, and today already feels like a week.

"Aren't you excited Mom? Aren't you excited that it is my birthday today, Mom?"

"I'm super excited," I answer as enthusiastically as one can be on five-and-a-half hours of sleep.

Thinking how glad I am that the party is at 12:00 noon and not a minute later my eyes check my watch, wow, 7:37 AM already. What is that they say about time flying?

I look up from the computer, set my love mug down on the coaster to my right, turn my eyes towards the window in front of me and look to the heavens.

"Thank you, God," I say, meaning it. Thank you for this boy who is so full of love. Thank you for this boy who at "one, one" only wants a $10.00 toy and will be over the moon with it. Thank you for this boy who has no ego, the purest soul on the planet, nothing but love shooting out of him at all times. Thank you for somehow thinking I am up to this challenge. I'm hoping you know more than I do, because it is now 7:40 AM, and I am already fantasizing about his bedtime."

"Mom! I almost forgot! I love you!" he says, eyes bright, smile wide, dimples deep.

"I love you, too, Wil, I'm so glad you were born! You're the best thing that ever happened to me," I answer, eyes bright, smile wide, wrinkles deep.

Carrie Wilson Link

THE THIRD NOBLE TRUTH:

Cessation of suffering is possible

Carrie Wilson Link

.

CHAPTER FIFTEEN

Five years ago my mother moved from this high desert country in the center of Oregon to Portland, in the Willamette Valley. She moved from this house, the only one she'd ever bought and lived in all by herself; into the rental house Ed and I still own. In exchange for rent we have use of this 1970's ranch-style house in the town of Sisters. Population 911. A number and a house used to call on for help.

She moved here needing a fresh start. The home became her house of healing. It became one I chose to come to, year after year, season after season. A home of fresh starts for me, too. It is my house these next few weeks. Just mine. No husband, no kids, no duties or responsibilities to anyone beyond myself. Ed and I had agreed: I needed a complete break. A rest. To stop.

Without these people, though, I am stymied. Forty-four-years-old and this is my first stab at self-care, the first time I am living alone, ever. Without the needs and demands of others I am at a loss for things to do. I've gone from one hundred miles per hour to zero, with no gradual decrease in my speed and intensity. Sudden brakes applied to a speeding train at the end of its track. I lurch and shake with the change of velocity. My body cannot be held still, my mind is even worse. I jump up with each new thought and impulse, moving constantly when there is nothing that truly requires my attention. I create things to do, because without a list and a calendar my days hold no meaning, no purpose. Without these guides telling me what to do and when to do them, I find little reason to get out of bed. Some days I hardly do, napping several hours a day and sleeping ten or more hours a night. I sleep like the dead. I am making up for lost time, or trying to lose time; I'm not sure which.

It feels right that while I am spending time here, in the

home my mother left behind to move closer to me. I am moving heaven and earth, literally, to be closer to her.

I thought that when I came here to be alone this time would help me understand my roles as mother and wife, the demands of which consume and exhaust me. I am surprised by how much of my time is spent understanding my role as daughter. Perhaps, it is simply because I am in my mother's space, space I would not have access to if it weren't for her. Perhaps, it is because until I break down and understand my evolving role as daughter, I will not understand my role as mother. Perhaps, it is more than her home I now have access to, even more than just her – is it possible that it is all of my ancestors? All that has been handed down to me either consciously or unconsciously? Maybe one of the biggest reasons I am here is to be more mindful of the place in history I take up, in the greater scheme of things.

It was suggested to me that I find a way to harness the energy of this ancient land, and the spirits of my mother and all my ancestors before her. An acquaintance trained in Eastern beliefs and ways of the soul, has proclaimed this land a holy place of healing, and with just a few slight tweaks, I can maximize the good energy that already abounds, and make it even stronger, more healing, holier. I am given instructions over e-mail. The juxtaposition of ancient ways being relayed through high tech means strikes me as wrong somehow. How far this is from mother-to-mother-to-mother through the generations. How splintered and disenfranchised it seems to hear from a friend of a friend, and with a few strokes on a keyboard miles away, I am given sacred information. What a metaphor for how far from my ancestors I am. Completely separated from their wisdom, their grace, their guidance.

Freshly showered, wearing a clean T-shirt and shorts, hair combed but left to dry on its own, face free from all make-up and wearing no jewelry, I walk back to the sliding glass door and survey my progress. I am making a grid, a rock formation according to specific directions.

I bend at the knees, "Let your legs do the work," my

mother's voice plays in my ear, "save your back!" Feet in her old sandals, hands in her forgotten gloves, pushing her old, once green wheelbarrow around her land, I stop the bending and teetering on the balls of my feet, hot June sun straight above and let go of the handles of the wheelbarrow.

From crouch to stand is beyond what I have the energy to do. And so I don't. I let myself fall. Simply let gravity take over where my strength has left off. I fall backwards, gently, letting the soft, dry land catch me.

Eyes at the sky with my hand making shade, I stop. Just like that. I don't push the wheelbarrow. I don't lift the rocks. I don't finish what I started. I stop.

I lie on my back, knees bent, legs splayed to make a "W" and I listen. It's so quiet here. So quiet I hear the birds, the wind, a dog barking far away, the air conditioner humming from inside the house. I've never wanted to stop before, never wanted to hear the quiet, make room for what it is trying to say, but I can't push it back for one more minute. The weight of the quiet is stronger than my will to silence it.

What I have always been afraid would happen if I stopped my perpetual movement, begins to happen. Tears slip under the dam, first one, then several, evaporating quickly on my cheeks. When they start to fall faster than the sun can dry them, I grab the bottom of my dirty T-shirt and dab them away.

The words on my T-shirt say "Joyful Heart," but the shirt is a liar and so am I. My heart is not full of joy. My heart is not full at all. My heart is a stranger to itself, empty, void. My head, that is what is full, full of noise and confusion and anger and lies. Grit in my ears, full of messages I am tired of recycling through on a continuous loop. A loop that threatens to clutch at my throat and choke the life right out of it.

Feelings I've pushed back want in now. The first wave to hit is from eleven years ago, right after Wil was born.

My tears and snot, sweat and soreness finally make it necessary to get up. I rise from my spot on the ground, look over at the house on my left, the mountains on my right, sun up above and the impression my body has left below. I've left impressions everywhere I've been in this lifetime. I back the wheelbarrow over the dented earth, scribbling the impression away.

Sliding open the glass door, I drop my dirty gloves on the throw rug, kick off the filthy sandals and remove all my clothes. There are no neighbors near enough to see me from their houses, and I am alone in this one. Not being seen is the best part about being here. I am invisible. I am anonymous. Total and complete solitude.

I walk down the hall to the bathroom, taking quick notice of the artwork I have chosen to hang there to replace the photographs my mother had hung. I have just one piece, centered perfectly, carefully chosen for its colors and message, "Let the Son in," bright yellow paint splashed to reveal an image of Pope John Paul II.

Once inside the bathroom, my eyes catch my grubby body in the mirror as I pull the curtain back and climb in the shower. The mirror tells a story. How very much my mother and I are alike.

CHAPTER SIXTEEN

It's another hot, sunny, gorgeous June day. Each day has a pattern of heat and light that offer me the structure I am looking for. There is a time perfect for coffee and meditation in the cool morning as the sun rises. I sit outside and watch the day come to be. If I wait until after 9:00 AM to go for a walk, it's too late, it'll be too hot and I'll be too miserable to get any benefit from the exertion. By 5:00 PM it has already started to cool and is another perfect time for sitting outside, drinking a Corona, a slice of lime wedged in the narrow neck of the clear bottle. Coffee in the morning, Corona in the evening, these times of quiet contemplation bookend my days in a way that lends support without stifling me. After "Beer O'Clock" it is time to open all the windows and doors, turn off the single air conditioning unit that sits in a hole in the wall where once a microwave belonged, and crank up the music. All day long I play chants, folk songs, soothing lullabies. When I cross over from workday to evening, an artificial line I've drawn to keep me feeling productive, the music turns to something that says, "time to party." My mood and energy lift as I take an imaginary marker and create another hash mark indicating I've done it. I've survived another day of this self-imposed and interminable solitude. This solitude that makes Sisters the best and the worst place in the world. Solitude that feeds me with stillness and robs me of absolutes.

This quiet, such a shock to the system after the constant noise and chaos of family. Even our Family Prayer Time is noisy and chaotic. After buying our house from the nuns, we have honored our promise to them to keep their spirits in the home. Ed and I worked to establish a routine that does just that, while combining what we love about Christianity and Buddhism, and putting them together in our own makeshift "practice." Wil loves this part of the day so much - there is no consideration of abolishing it, despite thirteen-year-old Jane's request for more time to primp before eighth grade.

"Are we having prayer today?" Wil asks, repeatedly, every single Monday, Tuesday, Thursday, and Friday mornings during the school year.

"Yes. We are having prayer today."

"What TIME are we having prayer today?" he persists.

"7:30, Sweet Love."

"10:30 AM EST?" he asks.

"Yes, 7:30 AM PST, 10:30 AM EST, Wil."

"Can I ring the gong when it is prayer time?"

"Yes, Wil, you can ring the gong."

"Can I get ready for prayer at 7:20 AM?"

"Yes. At 7:20 AM it would be very helpful if you got prayer ready."

"Will you tell me when it is 7:20?"

"Yes, I will tell you when it is 7:20."

"And then I will get prayer ready, right? At 7:20 I will get prayer ready? At 7:30 I will ring the gong, right?"

"Right."

"Can Big Bird come to prayer today at 7:30? Please? Can my little brother, Big Bird, come to prayer today at 7:30?"

At 7:20 AM, Wil pulls each of the four chairs that rest on the side of the periwinkle painted walls in the dining room, and scoots them up to the table. He moves the vase of fresh flowers and replaces the centerpiece with a candle on which Tibetan prayers are written. From the antique hat rack/umbrella stand he pulls off from a hook the small, velvet bag, which is home to over fifty "Angel Words," and places them at Ed's spot at the table. From where umbrellas might ordinarily rest, he grabs any combination of two of the following: *Warrior of the Light: A Manual, by* Paulo Coelho, *Be Still and Know: Reflections from Living Buddha, Living Christ,* by Thich Nhat Hanh, *Jesus and Buddha: The Parallel Sayings* by Marcus Borg, or *Buddha's Little Instruction Book,* by Jack Kornfield. Placing those also at Ed's spot, his job is nearly done.

He then yells at Ed, "IT IS TIME TO LIGHT THINGS, DAD!" Ed drops what he is doing to light the incense and the candle on the mantle, as well as the one in the center of the table.

Wil then moves to the bottom of the stairs after taking down the gong that also sits on the mantle and strikes it three times. Three. That serves to tell Jane, Ed and me that it is officially prayer time, and we are to skedaddle downstairs, quietly, prayerfully, and join him at the prayer table. Wil, already dressed in his school uniform, navy shorts and white polo uniform shirt, Jane in her uniform of khaki "skort" and white polo uniform shirt, Ed in his "out in the world" clothes, khakis and a golf shirt, me in my "I work from home" pajamas or sweats. Wil points out where each of our assigned seats are for the day, which seldom vary, but he "decides" none-the-less. He then pantomimes -- there is after all, no stray talking during prayer time -- until we all recognize by smiling or nodding the presence of Big Bird, Sully, Max, Stanley, Lucky or whoever his preferred "little brother" is for the day.

Although the stack of official sources lies by Ed, Jane and Wil take turns being "it." Wil is Monday and Thursday, Jane is Tuesday and Friday. Each day Wil argues over whose turn it is.

"I'M TUESDAY!" he argues, just to bug Jane, big twinkle in his eyes.

"DAAAAAAADDDDD, I'm Tuesday," Jane responds, out of habit and irritation.

I drop my head into my hands and try to re-focus, breathe, think to myself, this will be over soon. They will be out the door in just a few short minutes. You can do it, Carrie, you're on the home stretch. Ed, knowing whose turn it is and ignoring their inner game, pivots his body towards the predetermined person, and fans out all the angel words like he's holding a deck of playing cards. On his face is the "just take one" look.

"Pick," his actions say.

The point is to "divine" the card, to pick by not picking. Pick from the gut not from the mind, believing that whatever word is chosen is perfect for the day that lies ahead. Nine times out of ten, no matter how well we "shuffle," Wil selects "love" from the fan of cards.

"Oh! Love! I just LOVE love!" he says, kissing the tiny card over and over again, then pressing the tiny piece of laminated material firmly against his cheek.

On the rare occasion he does not "pick" love, he says, "I'm just going to pick one more, OK?" Then he scatters all the cards on the table until he eventually finds love, declares his love for love, and kisses the card enthusiastically.

Jane tends to draw Brotherhood/Sisterhood a lot. No accidents.

Then whoever's turn it is divines one of the two books selected for the day. Nine times out of ten, again, Wil lands on the same two pages from *Buddha's Little Instruction Book.*

"Blessings come from care, troubles come from carelessness," says the left-hand page. "If you do not care for each other, who will care for you?" says the right.

All four of us chant the words in a singsong voice, having heard them so many times they risk becoming a joke.

Then it is my turn. I divine a page from *Warrior of the Light: A Manual.* I read the words carefully and solemnly, as solemnly as one with bed head and sloppy pajamas is capable of. Nothing about my appearance says, "Listen to me, I've got it all figured out." I'm hoping the tone will compensate.

After I read I say, "The word of the Lord," and Ed, Jane and Wil reply with, "Thanks, be to God."

We then move into Prayers of the Faithful. This is not the time to make a wish. This is the time to be prayerful. No "That I get an A on my test" or "That it doesn't rain today" is allowed. No wishing those who are sick get "all better." We do not assert our will over that of the Divine's. We, Ed and I, try to use this chance to demonstrate gratitude.

"For Elmo, who is coming to school with me today in my backpack, that he has a good day," Wil says.

"Lord, hear our prayer," we respond in unison.

"For Mrs. Murphy's eye," Jane usually says, praying that her beloved teacher's long-term vision troubles and pain will be relieved.

"Lord, hear our prayer," we reply.

"Thank you for our family," Ed says.

"Lord, hear our prayer," we say.

"For all those we love that are sad, alone, hurt or afraid, we pray to the Lord," I am most likely to say.

"Lord, hear our prayer," they answer automatically.

Wil almost always pulls out the name of some random person and has us praying for them all day. We do. He knows stuff. We don't question the method to his madness. Jane consistently prays for those whom her class has been asked to pray for, and always, we pray for her friend and ours, Abby, who is living with cystic fibrosis. Wil always adds, "... and her whole family" if that part gets left off. He understands that when one person in the family is "ill," it affects the whole family.

Then, whoever is in charge leads us in our favorite leftover from kindergarten prayer, "Open Our Eyes." We love the kindergarten teacher both kids had and thank her all the time for having the kids memorize this perfect prayer. If I were left on a deserted island and could only say one prayer for the rest of my life, this would be it:

"Lord, open our eyes to see beauty,
Open our ears to hear truth,
Open our mouths to speak kindness,
Open our minds to seek wisdom,
And open our hearts to love."

Wil thrusts his "baby brother" at one of us and orders us to "help them." Obediently, we move their plush limbs in the sign of the cross over each sense, just as we do for ourselves, tying our basic Christian/Catholic practices to our woo-woo ways.

We then join hands, Big Bird too, and sing "Amen."

"Aaaaaaaamen, aaaaaaaamen, aaamen, aaaamen, aaaaamen," we sing. While clasped hands are being pulled apart, Wil's blowing out the candles, Jane already has her hands on her cell phone desperately needing to make her transportation to school arrangements, Ed is already ordering that coats and shoes be put on and I am already relieved that our togetherness is over for the day. Before I let them officially "go," I add in, "Go make a difference!"

"Amen," I say to myself. I too, want to make a difference and staying in Portland amidst that chaos was not making a difference, it was perpetuating everything but.

CHAPTER SEVENTEEN

I sit at my mother's table this morning. I drink from her coffee cup, rest the cup on her coaster, grab the cream from her old refrigerator. I look at the scratches and nicks on this antique table. How many times did my mother sit right where I am sitting and do just what I am doing? Settle herself into her day, into her skin, into her part of the collective? How did all these scratches and nicks earn their way onto this table and into the story of this woman?

I open her sliding glass door to let my friends the quail and deer distract and inspire me. When the blue jays finish every last bit of their seed, I slide into my mother's old left-behind, too big, very stained, hideous yet super comfortable sandals and walk the twenty feet to the feeder to re-fill it for the day.

Back at the table, I pick up my coffee and look around. It's impossible to feel too far away from my mother while spending my days in her home. Even if she'd fully moved out before I'd temporarily moved in her energy would still fill the space entirely. She didn't really ever move out though, she just took a few things with her and started over in Portland. Her things are everywhere. There is still food in the cupboards, flour, salt, baking powder - "staples" she would call them. In the refrigerator is her favorite salad dressing, a light balsamic vinaigrette. Her blue terrycloth robe hangs on its hook behind the bathroom door. I half expect her to walk though the oak door she selected any minute and say, "I'm home! Surprise!"

Slowly I've moved more and more of my personal items to this house. Five years ago it looked just the way she left it. Today, it looks like a home we share, two roommates taking turns in the house that is their one true home.

With both my feet in this home now and both hers in Portland, I slide my feet into her shoes and head outside to continue my work on the grid. I am anxious for anything that has hope of harnessing and directing some of the energy surging through me. If this grid does that, it will be well worth the heat and exhaustion that building it causes.

I pull out the printed e-mail and read out loud:

"Using rocks from the land, lay them in straight lines from each of the corners of the house, creating diagonal lines, and the four north, south, east and west points of the house, creating straight lines. There will be a radiant, sunbeam effect when you are done."

My father's voice pops in my head, "Measure twice, cut once. Plan your work, then work your plan," but my mother's impulsiveness and need to move is stronger, drowning out the voice that says, "You'll be sorry! You'll have to do this all again! Well begun is half done!"

With no plan at all, I head back outside, grab hold of the wheelbarrow and continue to gather rocks from the three-quarter acre of land. When the wheelbarrow gets too heavy to move, I start to concede that perhaps I should have listened to my father's voice rather than behave like my mother. I've become the worst of both of them, the best of neither. No wonder those two never made it as a couple. Now they live inside of me, and "we" are not making it as a couple either, always at odds with ourselves - reason and logic fighting with obsessions and compulsions. My father, buried in the ground for eleven years, divorced from my mother twenty before that, still has a bone to pick with her and I've allowed myself to become the tool he uses to poke. My psyche is nothing but bumps and bruises from all the poking and picking.

Again, I drop the wheelbarrow from my grip, letting it fall with a soft thud on the ground. Again, I stop what I am doing and put body to earth. Again, I try to stop the tapes running through my head, letting in the voice from inside me that has so long been stifled. Lying down, letting down, resting and reconsidering my next move.

I take off the Nike cap on my head and use it to cover my face from the sun. Underneath its smelly fabric, I close my eyes and try to experience just being with myself. Lying flat on my back, arms and legs spread as if to make a snow angel, I breathe and try to just be.

My fingers rub the embroidered letters, Nike, and I'm flooded with all my connections to that word, and that place, Nike, where Ed and I fell in love.

I decide to make a dirt angel, an angel of the earth. Arms spread wide, I use my wings to fly, right here, on this mother, Earth.

I finally concede that yes, I need a system for getting all these rocks gathered and spread across the land. The idea of forcing the wheelbarrow around and just eyeballing where the rocks should go proved ill begotten. I'd done three such "rows" yesterday before letting loose with a string of salty language and calling it a day.

Today I'm all plan and purpose. I find a couple of old buckets in the garage and taking the smaller of the two, I gather up the first four feet of row one from yesterday. Scanning the shelves in my mother's garage I find twine and head back outside. The day is not too hot yet, I have all the doors and windows open. I select the perfect CD for this work, "ReTURNING" by Jennifer Berezan. I move the player as far as the cord will stretch -- placing it in the open kitchen window -- approximately the halfway mark of the house, and turn the volume to high.

Soothing, peaceful music fills the air and my heart. Words in different languages, all with the same message of healing and returning, to the mother of us all. I will return to this mother, Earth. I will return to my role as a mother. I will return to my own mother. I will return to the Holy Mother, too. But just one at a time. Today it is to the earth I will return.

I've decided the front is where I will start. It seems appropriate. I march myself and the twine forward until I reach a ponderosa pine that feels far enough, just on the edge of the property line. Realizing I've nothing with which to cut the twine, I drop it and begin running back into the house to fetch scissors. I catch myself running, hurrying for no reason at all, and force my steps to slow, to feel the earth beneath them.

I am returning.

CHAPTER EIGHTEEN

With each rock I pick up and place, a stone in my being moves too, adjusts, shakes loose the others. Is it any wonder that so many of my other relationships follow this same rocky path?

While the physical labor involved in building this grid feels strenuous, my mind begins to rest deeply with new insights.

On my mind now are questions with no answers, perhaps, but I rest in the unknowing. Like pearls being turned over and over inside the oyster, I turn the questions over and over in my mind and my heart. Just turning them seems to be enough. With each revolution there is new wisdom.

I think how rocks break down, weather and years turning boulders into rocks, rocks into sand. Sand that finds its way into the mouth of an oyster. The mucous and warm dampness of the oyster turning the sand over and over until it becomes a pearl. How very much like oysters women are, taking the grit of our lives and turning it into beauty. From our body we take the male's seed, smaller than a grain of sand, and in our warm and mucous filled center we turn this seed over and over again until great beauty, a miracle, a child, is formed.

From pearls to oysters to children... my mind turns with this new knowing, revolutions becoming revelations.

This is the time to turn my story, my life, the gently planted pearls of wisdom from within and without, and see all sides. What is true? What is true about those truths, and whose truths are they?

When I am in Portland, I have a dear friend Kathleen with whom I walk. We're on year nine of our multi-weekly walks. The time together is sacred, true friends bringing fresh breath to each of our lives, our relationship, and our bodies. We've solved a lot of the world's problems as we march in perfect synchronicity. We've shared our heartbreaks, our joys, our struggles. This is time I look forward to and guard against any intrusion. When I am alone, though, I find every reason in the book to skip the walk. Together the time flies, alone it seems to move backwards. I've been here in Sisters two weeks now. I am restless for something to happen. All this solitude is starting to make me crazy. I'm about to call the whole thing off, pack up and return to Portland, thank my husband Ed for pitching in and formally relieve him of all domestic duties. I'll just pick right up right where I left off. If I get home soon, maybe nothing will have slipped through the cracks there. I've still got time to catch what Ed has left to fall. I still have time to rescue everyone from a life without my orchestration. I still have time. But if I stay here much longer the kids will run out of their medicine. Groceries will run out. Beds will need to be changed, appointments will need to be made, really important things will not happen.

That is my fear.

No, that is not my fear. My fear is that nothing will fall through the cracks. That I am expendable.

Feet move forward while my thoughts reach back to Portland. By this time, Ed has already made breakfast for Wil. Making the breakfast is not hard, you could do it your sleep, since it is exactly the same every single day. What makes it hard is that unless you get up and fully caffeinate by 5:30 AM, Wil is going to wake up first, and the volume, intensity and demands of the day throw you into a tailspin that takes the rest of the day from which to recover.

For thirteen years, I've been the primary parent, the one who stays at home and doesn't have to "work." I've been the one who gets up in the middle of the night with a sick or crying child, doesn't go to bed until everyone is tucked in and is up when the first one starts to crow. I've been the one to cook, clean, nurse, tend, feed and properly medicate. I've been the driver to all appointments, researcher of all disorders and solver of all problems. I've been the scheduler, keeper of all data, milestones, and memories. I've been the preparer of all parties, shopper of all gifts, liaison between the kids and the outside world. Always and only me. I imagine the morning Ed and Wil must be having by now.

"What kind of toast do you want this morning, Wil?" Ed asks.

"GARLIC!!" Wil answers emphatically, complete with dramatic arm gestures.

Ed opens the pantry, pushes his glasses back up from where they have slid down his nose and grabs the loaf of bread, grabbing the first two slices his fingers touch.

"I do not like those pieces!" Wil yells as his eyes spy the end slices.

Taking two center pieces from the rounded loaf, Ed puts them in balance in the toaster oven. One push of the on button gives Ed just enough time to locate the softened butter, a knife and the twelve-ounce shaker of garlic salt before the button pops up and round two begins.

Ed grabs two plastic plates from the third shelf down in the pantry. One is for the crusts which can be any plate at all, one is for the actual toast; that one must be fuchsia with white polka dots.

Toast comes out, gets flipped over and put back in, in reverse order. Another push of the button. Ed fills his coffee cup and is back over to the toast making area before the button springs up the second time.

"DAD! IT'S DONE!" Wil yells. Long thin legs, all muscle, steadily kick the side of the counter while the whole process takes place. Humming, singing, talk of the day carries on without pause.

"Are you picking me up at 3:15 today, Dad?"

"Yes" Ed answers, eyes on the toast. He carefully butters both pieces so that the garlic salt will stick properly.

"How come you are picking me up at 3:15 today, 6:15 PM Eastern?"

"Because Mom is gone," Ed says as he cuts the crusts off each piece, slicing them both in half and gingerly moving the good pieces to the preferred plate. If they stay on the original plate condensation will accumulate, thus rendering the toast inedible. Ed sprinkles the garlic salt evenly and expertly on the toast, handing it to Wil with a flourish, grabbing a piece of rejected crust and calling that "breakfast" for himself.

"THANK YOU!" Wil says, already ripping piece number one into bite-sized pieces and stuffing them into his mouth. Humming, kicking and chewing he asks, "What time is Jane waking up?"

"7:00, Wil."

"Why does she wake up at 10:00 AM Eastern?" he asks, simultaneously sneezing from all the extra garlic salt he's sneaked on his toast while Ed blinked. He wipes his eyes with his garlicky hands, rubbing salt into the eye and causing it to tear.

"Let me wipe the salt from your eyes, Wil," Ed pleads.

"NO!" Wil replies. "MYOB, Dad! My eyes do not have salt in them! My eyes are fine! Can't you just forget about the salt in my eyes?"

He grabs for the garlic salt again as Ed admonishes, "That's enough!"

"DAD! Can you just let me have my garlic salt? Can you just go upstairs and let me have my garlic salt? Can you just stop worrying about the garlic salt?"

I check my watch and see that it's 8:45 AM. By now Ed has been up with Wil for three hours. This brings me back to the house, my walk is over and I'm smiling with the twisted hope that as I am just starting my day, eager for what lies ahead, Ed is already counting down to bedtime.

CHAPTER NINETEEN

As my feet return to the driveway where they began, my eyes look up and smile at the Tibetan prayer flags I've strewn all around the front. Where once Christmas lights hung, small hooks now hold flags from another land. It takes three sets to reach from one end of the house's eaves to the other. Two more sets are stretched and tied to ponderosa pines on either side of the driveway, two more doing the same thing in the back, their five colors blowing and flapping in the wind.

From left to right the colors are yellow, green, red, white and blue, representing earth, water, fire, cloud and sky. Then the five colors repeat themselves, again and again until all you really notice when you look is the brightness and the feeling you get of being an integral part of something bigger "out there".

On top of each flag are the markings of Buddhist prayers. Like the colors, those prayers repeat themselves. Simple prayers, blowing their blessings out into the world as the wind blows through their colored cotton rectangles.

The Tibetans believe the wind carries these blessings to all sentient beings. Sentient means having the ability to sense or feel. I believe the trees whose trunks have these flags attached are sentient. They must be. How else do you explain that when I look at them they seem to sway towards me? And what about those big, puffy white clouds that look like a kindergartner drew them with a crayon? I believe those are sentient, too. When I lie on my back outside and stare at them they appear to move in direct accordance with my thoughts.

Each color is symbolic, to both the Tibetans and to me. The yellow flags are earth. I am out-of-touch with the fact I'm on the earth when I'm in Portland, but here I am constantly aware. I feel small, yet big, and part of something even bigger here. In the weeks I've been here, I've moved in sync with the sun, moon, heat, and cold. I have not fought against it, but worked with it. Harmony.

The green flags are water. There is a fountain that sings to me while I write, sleep, meditate, procrastinate. It sits right outside the front door and I hear its rhythmic whisperings from all parts of the small house. The earth beneath my feet is so dry it's dust. I don't water the yard, only the small plants I've planted, herbs, hearty sentient beings meant to smell and make me feel good.

The red flags are fire. I have smudged this land, nearly lighting the whole place on fire with errant sparks from the burning sage. I have lit tea lights and tall glass candles with the Virgin de Guadalupe's image wrapped around. They're $1.58 at the grocery store. These candles burn first thing in the morning and again at dusk. The lighting and extinguishing of flame is a ritual I have come to love and find comforting, rhythmic and peaceful. I am not alone or in the dark when I am surrounded by the light of these candles, the light of Mother Mary.

Clouds are represented by the white flags. This summer has brought day after day of mostly cloudless skies. It's one of the things I like most about this climate; when it's time to rain it's cloudy, when it's time to shine it's not - so unlike Portland, which always has clouds. At times during the year it feels there is nothing beyond the low ceiling of those clouds. It's easy to forget there is a sun when I'm in Portland. It's easy to forget things are bigger than I am when I'm in Portland. It's easy to forget this cloudless feeling of vast possibilities when I'm in Portland. There is a closed-in feeling that comes from living in the Willamette Valley. There is a closed-in, claustrophobic feeling just thinking about Portland, all the obligations and responsibilities. All the stress and strain. The permanency of it all. There is a closed-in feeling that comes from living in the cage I've built around my heart, home and life there.

My crazy life is what I am trying to make sense of now. For thirteen years the craziness was so active I couldn't find a way out, but now, finally there is some breathing room. I breathe now, deeply and purposefully as I focus on the blue prayer flags. Blue, my favorite, the color of my eyes and those of my children, the color from which I look out and see the world, the color of water, of cool, rest and peace. The color of Mary. The blue of the prayer flag represents the sky itself. The sky is the limit. Just looking at those flags I believe that. When I was a little girl a small poster hung above my bed, a gift from my mom. "Women hold up half the sky," the poster said. A crudely drawn childlike image of a woman, arms outstretched, with the sky split right in two, held firmly in place by her capable arms.

Perhaps with me here, Ed there, all I have to do is hold up my half. I can let the other half go. Let him hold up half. Some things might slip through the cracks, but that will need to be OK with me, I guess. Holding up the whole sky has grown tiresome. If I only have half to hold, maybe I can hold on twice as long?

Perhaps this was what was trying to come through as I paced the house. I smile at the prayer flags. I smile at the ponderosa pines. I smile at myself, and not just half of myself, either. My whole self.

I'm on the last straight line of the grid, the one from the garage corner out to the end of the property on the east end. Up and down with my knees, arms reaching for the right rocks from the bucket at my feet. I've created a medium, small, small, big pattern for the rocks in the other lines of the grid and this one must follow suit. Sometimes this attention to detail requires that I keep re-filling the bucket, finding myself "out" of the next piece of the puzzle. But I am careful to do this the "New Carrie" way, slow and steady.

Medium, small, small, big. Repeat. My sport bra rides up and with my gloved hand I yank it back down. My feet are dirty from wearing the sandals and I find this too, part of the "New Carrie" way, embracing the dirt, the wrongness of doing this yard work in sandals, instead of proper footwear. "That's a good way to break a toe," I hear my father's voice say. I smile at my own inconsistencies, slow and steady precision with one aspect of my project, half-assed and careless with another. I'm getting a big kick out of myself, alone here in Sisters. I'm finding my own company delightful these days, actually making myself laugh out loud at times, sharing inside jokes with myself.

While placing "big" in its place, my eyes catch something blue in the periphery. I leave "big," taking steps towards blue. I pick up an old, small, plastic square-shaped food container and find blue to be the lid to its clear bottom. Cracked and missing a key part, a necklace dangles from plastic. Prying open the lid I pull the string of pearl beads out from the top and turn them over in my hand. Throwing gloves to the ground with both parts of the box, I blow hard to shake loose the first layer of dirt covering the beads.

Walking into the kitchen and turning the faucet on, I hold the necklace under the stream until the brown falling from below turns to clear. I turn over the story of this necklace, these pearl beads, this plastic storage container and how it showed up today of all days. Long after I've recalled they were once my mother's and she gave them to Jane to play with when Jane was young, I am still struggling to discern how I could have possibly walked by them all these years and never noticed.

Could Jane have buried them, like a treasure? Did all my digging up of rocks unbury them? Did an animal find them and move them from their original place? It has to be ten years since Jane last played with these. Have they been out here all along, right under my nose just waiting until I was ready to have them revealed?

Last night I dreamt of pearls. I was a diviner of pearls' authenticity. I had the only teeth in the land that could determine their genuineness. People came from all over to hand me their strands, have me rub them across my teeth and give the official pronouncement, "Fake!" or "Real!" I shouted with ultimate authority.

Just this morning, coffee in my hands and soothing mantras playing in my headphones, I sat not ten feet from where these pearls lay and meditated on my dream of fake and real.

I shiver, despite the climbing temperature, with this knowing feeling that falls on me. I am on to something here. I must press forward. I must finish what I've started. This "nothingness" I've got going is quite something.

CHAPTER TWENTY

Going north to south you've got your Faith, Hope and Charity. Mountains, that is. The town of Sisters is named after these three majestic beauties. Everyone knows there are three of them, but most commonly they are referred to as the North, Middle and South Sister. I think to do so though is to minimize how wonderful they are.

The Three Sisters are part of the Cascade Mountain Range. In between the mountains, a valley has formed -- the Willamette Valley, in which I have lived all my life. Another mountain in the range is Broken Top, just south of Charity. There is something about the way Broken Top looks that makes you either stare, or look quickly away, like a person with an obvious deformity. A huge chunk of it is simply missing. I choose to believe it was hanging around Charity for a few millennia that got to him, until one day he simply willed volcanic activity to yank off his top and bestow it upon a less fortunate mountain in the range.

South of the broken one, stands Bachelor. He's just there, in all his perfect mountain way. He is gorgeous, a real looker. He is just what you'd hope to find in a mountain. He is tall, handsome, steady, sturdy, and a lot of fun. People travel from miles around to ski the slopes of Mt. Bachelor. He gets all the glory, all the good resorts, all the attention. Personally, I have a small crush on Broken Top. I always go for the underdog.

Except when I married, I broke my own rule and went for the winner. I went for one with trophies, the tall, handsome, lots of fun guy.

Ed, my Mt. Bachelor, recognizes my deep need to rest, relax, and recover from the thirteen years of intense parenting responsibilities. For these few weeks he is going to do everything, relieve me of all parenting responsibilities. He has adjusted his schedule to work at home. It's not that he's been an inactive father, he's been willing to and does help, but for reasons I'm just starting to understand, it's been "easier" for me to just do most things. As a result, I've struggled with headaches, depression, anxiety, stomach distress, and two giant breast lumps. I see now that those were all symptoms of a problem, and not only didn't I understand what the problem was, I didn't understand whose problem it was.

After "Mt. Bachelor" talked up the whole "You go and rest" plan for the umpteenth time, I agreed. What I said was, "OK." What I didn't say was, "I'm afraid if I leave, I'll never come back."

Many times a day I stop whatever it is I'm doing, and look up, eyes to the heavens, and scan for my friends, the Three Sisters. We say, "The mountains aren't out today," or "All the mountains are out today" around here, as if the mountains are the ones choosing to be seen or unseen, not the weather that either obscures or illuminates their majesty.

For forty-four years, I've chosen to come out or not come out, allowing the weather of those around me to determine the extent to which I shine. A life of skilled eggshell walking has taken its toll. I am angry. I am bitter, and deeply resentful. I look up at Broken Top right there next to the Three Sisters - Faith, Hope and Charity – all on my side.

"Show me what to do," I beg them.

On my altar I have the pearl necklace I found outside. Each day during meditation I take the necklace off the altar and hold it between my fingers like a mala. Each bead is rubbed while I say to myself, "Forgive, forgive, forgive," one "forgive" per bead. Although I practice this forgiveness meditation, there is still something in me that nags with the thought, "But if you forgive, you are letting all those people who hurt you off the hook." I know that nagging comes from my ego; that it is not for them that I offer forgiveness. What I believe philosophically and am trying to get my ego to go along with is the idea that *I* deserve the relief forgiveness offers. My back has borne the burden for so long my shoulders sag under the weight. I love the imperfection of this necklace, the tackiness even. I want to be more like that necklace. Tacky, flawed, honest. Not the buffed and polished woman everyone in Portland thinks I am, the woman who smiles, writes thank you notes on personally engraved paper, volunteers for everything and keeps a perfect home. Tacky. I want to be cheaper, bolder, more garish, far less cultured. Cultured hasn't worked for me.

I move back to my altar, pick up the fake pearl necklace and hold it loosely in my hands. My story is like this necklace; full of knots, binding ties, thread worn thin, beads that show rust and have out-served their purpose. They no longer hold the necklace together, but threaten to destroy it.

What would the future be like for all of us if I were to forgive my mother? Forgive both my fathers? Forgive my husband? Forgive myself? If I can wash clean the slate, isn't that the best gift I can bestow on my daughter? Total freedom? A life that is hers with nothing from mine, my mother's or my grandmother's to drag along behind her like a ball and chain?

I take the pearl necklace, slip into my mother's shoes and begin to walk the land. One grid at a time, north, south, east, west and the four corners. Holding loosely to the strand I let my story drop as I walk, one rock at a time. Step, step, step, drop. Medium, small, small, big. A pattern. A pattern of forgiveness.

I feel a vice on my head, my eyes struggle to focus. One look at the crack of light coming under the shade and I wince in pain. Looks like it's going to be a migraine day. This is how they all start out. I wake up with a bad headache that just gets worse and worse until it goes away in two days if I'm lucky, four or five if I'm not.

Gingerly putting one foot in front of the other, I make my way to the bathroom. The coldness of the concrete bathroom floor hits my bare feet, adding further assault to my tuning fork body, highly strung and ready to screech at the slightest touch. I wash my hands and face, brush my teeth, and swallow two Advil and two aspirin with yesterday's leftover water still in the glass. I grope my way to the kitchen, down a Cliff Bar and go back to bed. I will not let this headache get the best of me; I will nip it in the bud.

I fall back asleep and when my eyes again open, my headache is dulled enough that I make my way courageously to the coffee maker and my white notepad. I sit on the couch, both legs under me, and write with my non-dominant hand while I wait for the coffee. My left hand writes the words, "Please help me." That's funny, I think to myself, I wasn't aware I needed help, but my psyche seems to feel otherwise. I uncross my legs, get up, and jump a little on legs that have begun to fall asleep. On tingly legs I walk the few short steps to the kitchen, fling open the cupboard and choose carefully which mug I will use today. My morning coffee has all the dogma and ritual of a well-established religion. Deciding it is a red love mug kind of day, I open the refrigerator; pour in half and half with the left hand, right hand pouring the coffee. Pour and wait, pour and wait, pour and wait, if done properly there is no need for a spoon, one mixes with the other in perfect synchronicity.

Perhaps that is the help I am asking for, retroactive help. But can I let go of the past? Can I make room for new life?

For the last few months I've been obsessed with the work and wisdom of Carl Jung. I've always had an active dream life, but never taken the time to record my dreams like I've heard you are supposed to. Now I've got the time. Jung believed all aspects of our dreams represent parts of ourselves, so I apply this awareness to my daily routine, and diligently wake up each morning and write down my dreams. I then spend much of the day pulling the dreams apart in my mind, to discover hidden or misunderstood aspects of myself.

In one of Jung's books he says, "Every mother contains her

daughter in herself and every daughter her mother and every mother extends backwards into her mother and forwards into her daughter."

I strip down and grab hold of my mother's shower curtain, scooting it over before climbing in. My eyes rest on the rod, and an old image pops in. We always had my mom's pantyhose hanging from our shower curtain rods growing up. How many of her other routines and rituals do I know by heart and without any awareness replicate perfectly today?

Maybe there is a way to have new with the old, maybe I can have a new way of being with the "old" set of problems. Maybe the problems, and I, don't have to go away but merely be looked at from a different perspective? Maybe, in fact, they aren't problems at all.

I climb out of the shower, towel off, dress and sit down at the kitchen table. I jot down these ideas, draw a web of related thoughts, watch as circles and lines are drawn from one thought to the other, connecting.

CHAPTER TWENTY-ONE

The view from the table provides its fair share of distractions. There are hummingbirds that need to be fed special nectar that I laboriously mix each morning. This requires that I pour six rounded teaspoons of something that looks a lot like red Jell-O mix into the narrow throat of the feeder bottle. Next I fill the bottle with warm water, plug the hole with my thumb and shake *gently*. I've learned the hard way that this nectar leaves a nasty red stain on the kitchen floor, which becomes a mixed blessing, as cleaning the floor is one more way I can stay busy. I then attach the base to the feeder, walk with one hand underneath to catch the drips, only turning it back right side up after I am safely outdoors. That kills a good five to ten minutes every day.

I've got a large bird feeder that hangs from a Ponderosa Pine tree in the back. I hang it extra low so the deer can come and snack from it too. The blue jays are the greediest, and after them the squirrels. The blue jays are also the messiest and pickiest, scattering the seeds that are not quite up to par all over the ground below. That's where the quail come in. I've got two sets of quail coming, two families, I guess. The mother and father are easy enough to distinguish by their subtle and flagrant colors, respectively. There must be some friends or relatives that tag along too, though, and all their little chicks. I can't swear, but I think there are thirteen babies. They scurry along the ground so fast I can't get a good headcount. The other quail family also has thirteen, I think, and the only way I know they are a different family is the babies are bigger. I've researched quail, and learned they are ground birds. They *can* fly, but they prefer not to. I like that in a bird. No need to show off, just a good skill to have in case it's necessary to take off in a pinch.

With any luck I can fill the feeder twice in one day. If I fill it right when I wake up, I can count on it being empty and in urgent need of filling again around 5:00 PM. With all the long hours of daylight, this provides me endless entertainment, and obviously, little time for anything else.

When I am out of excuses and do force my fingers back to my circles and lines that have filled a page of my notepad, I turn the page and begin to write and write, without censoring myself. I envy the lives of the deer, squirrel and birds that live on the other side of the glass.

When I'm done being jealous of wildlife, I turn on my computer and check for e-mails. There's one from Ed:

"Wil did it again. After a very long afternoon with him, we were playing on the play structure at the park. I was holding him so he could see how long he could hang from the monkey bars. He could see it in my eyes and in my body language; I was shot. He made full eye contract, threw in a twinkle and his cute smile, pointed to his chest and said, 'You live right in here, buddy.'"

And I go back to gratitude for being human.

It's too cold to get up. I choose this morning to record my dreams while remaining in the warmth of my bed with a down comforter pulled up to just below my chin. Fall is coming, I can't kid myself, the time to return home is fast approaching - the chill in the air is my proof.

I adjust the pillows, scoot myself around to stay warm and pick up the notepad.

I write down my dream of fish out of water, gerbils trying to free themselves from my tight grasp, bunnies too fat to move immobilized by over feeding, over indulgence, too many treats.

A part of me feels like a fish out of water. The small animal part of me wants to be released. The over-indulged part has immobilized me.

It is time to release my old stories. Permanently. The "I am a victim" story. The "Everyone else is the problem" story. The

"I live in a cage story." This is what those dreams mean to me. I put down the notepad, and scrunch down further into the warmth of the bed, eyes to the window to see what kind of light is trying to sneak in. The sun has not yet risen. There is no light seeping around the edges of the window shade.

There is light seeping in around me, though. Something I'm doing must be working. I feel better today, more hopeful, optimistic, clearer, brighter. I see the options before me and they feel like just that, options, not dead ends. Is it all the sleep? The clear mountain air? Time? Could all this deep processing be producing fruit?

I swing my legs over the sides of the bed, slide into my slippers and grope in the closet for a sweatshirt. One with a hood would be best. I am not taking any time for grooming today, but something's got to be done with this hair if I have any plan of leaving the house. Fortunately, the only plan I have is to leave this bedroom right now, get my butt in a chair and send Ed an e-mail – let him know my day of return. Start the process.

I think I've spent a total of one hour on grooming this summer and going back to make-up and hairstyling seem like reasonable "cons" on my list of reasons to return to Portland ASAP. There are a few other cons on the list, such as how am I going to re-enter chaos and keep the peace I've acquired while being alone? How am I going to blend into the story Ed, Jane and Wil have maintained while I was away? How will I handle the "new" way they do things if it's not the way I would do them, but it still works?

With my release of control, Ed has managed to fully toilet train Wil. I got Wil to pee in the toilet at age five, but since then I've been unable to convince him the toilet is where he needs to poop. Since I've been gone Ed has succeeded on that front.

Bigger than that though is the victim thing again. If Ed *does* have everything running smoothly without me, maybe he would have done it that much sooner if I'd invited it? Asked for it? Possibly even made a scene and demanded it? Probably.

I sit with my journal and try the non-dominant hand exercise again. It is believed that our psyches, our unconscious yet active thoughts, are given voice when we write with our non-dominant hand. I've been doing this for a few months now and it works for me. The first time I tried this I intended to write, "I need to be needed," but what I wrote was, "I need to be noted."

So with my journal and a big fat marker, the kind preschoolers use, I write the question in my journal using the dominant hand, my right, and then switch the marker to my non-dominant hand, the left. The question is: "Why do I hate to admit I am wrong?" My left hand answers, "I hate to admit I am wrong because I want people to like me and approve of me. If I admit I'm wrong, then I'm not perfect to them anymore."

There it is.

There's the theme of perfection again. A theme I say I've fought against, something I hate to be told I am, perfect. But actually what I am most afraid of is being discovered as imperfect. It's hard being flawed in a cultured world, hard to know which is more true, a perfect but fake pearl, or a flawed but real one.

CHAPTER TWENTY-TWO

I grab the little white stool that doubles as an end table and go outside. I climb up on the stool and tug at the Tibetan prayer flags strung along the lines of the house. This house is in a neighborhood with an association that likes codes and covenants. Christmas lights are fine, Tibetan prayer flags are not. They are too colorful; they do not blend in with the natural surroundings. Keeping them up all summer has been my silent rebellion. It's my act of passive aggression. It's the latent teenager energy that I never got to express. I get a little kick out of myself each time I pull into the driveway between two sets of prayer flags that greet me at the end.

But as with any good rebellion, you've eventually got to give it up. Today is the day I return to my family and taking down these outward signs of my independence here is part of that process. With each tug, tug, fold and gathering of the flags I remove there is a matching tug in my heart.

I am anxious to see Ed, Jane and Wil again. Anxious good and anxious bad. I love them with my whole heart. Is there any part of my heart left for me, if they are taking up the whole thing?

While I tug at the flags, I reflect again at the significance and order of their colors: blue for sky, white for clouds, red for fire/sun, green for vegetation/water and yellow for earth/soil. It is believed that they bring balance and harmony to where they hang and to wherever their prayers are blown. Harmony and balance, harmony and balance, I chant to myself as I tug and fold, tug and fold.

With one hand I hold the prayer flags I've tugged loose and with the other I shade my eyes and look at that sky. Just look. That sky goes on and on. That sky I'm looking at now stretches itself all the way to Portland. Like the prayer flags tied between trees, this sky stretches between my two lives, this one of solitude, to the one in Portland, the one of family, community, friends, reality.

If the sky can stretch from here to there, so can I. I can find a way to bridge my two ways of being. I can find a way to take this life of solitude, peace, quiet, no demands, and stretch it to my life, which is full of the needs of others.

With my black ten-year-old Honda CR-V packed to the gills, I pull out of the garage, slide the garage door down and give the lock a final turn. Click. Just like that, I am locking up this house and all the time I've spent here, all I've learned here, all I've worked through here. Click. Lock. Done.

"Goodbye, Sisters!" I shout at the sky. "Hello, Portland."

I jump back in the car and I'm off. I'm on my way home, headed due west. The Native Americans believe the west represents protection. I'm leaving the east, representative of new beginnings and enlightenment and heading towards protection, family. Like the click of the garage door, something clicks into place for me, too. Perhaps I have learned all I am supposed to learn from my Summer of Solitude. SOS. I am now ready to pick up and continue learning the value of family and protection.

I grow more and more anxious mile after mile. I have scarcely seen or spoken to anyone in my immediate or extended family all summer. I don't know how I will be received. I don't know what damage I've caused that might be hard or impossible to repair. I shall soon find out. In three hours, to be precise.

Check school supply lists against inventory. Measure kids for uniforms and place order. Check which plants have survived inside and out and replace accordingly. These are the thoughts ping-ponging in my brain as I keep my hands on the wheel at ten and two, glancing in my rearview mirror every few seconds just like I learned in driver's ed. I can follow rules, no problem there.

Carrie Wilson Link

FOURTH NOBLE TRUTH:

The cessation of suffering comes from the Middle Way

CHAPTER TWENTY-THREE

With the kids back in school now, my transition home has become easier. Ed resumes leaving for the office every morning as the kids leave for school and I now have the house to myself from 8:00 AM - 3:00 PM each day. I find myself using all the same distraction techniques I used in Sisters. I have a tremendous need to sort, purge, organize, and clean. I methodically go through the house; every drawer, cupboard and closet is fair game. The sight of all our excess sickens me. I literally cannot look at it without feeling ill. I promise myself I will reduce it all by half. I will make space in this house for openness, clarity, newness - expansiveness of thought and being.

I decide to start in the basement and work my way up. This decision feels right, symbolic, important to me at some base level. So with Jane's CD player, garbage bags and grubby clothes, I get to work. Dar Williams, Anna Nalick, and Antje Duvekot, women artists I've only recently been introduced to, as well as old favorites like Mary Chapin Carpenter, Shawn Colvin and the Indigo Girls play on as I work.

"Goodwill," "Recycle," "Garbage," say the three tubs in the center area of the basement. Concrete floor painted red, chipped in most places, rough spots and cracks, dips and slopes make the surface an extra challenge as well as cold and hard. I put knees to floor and hold still on the firm, cool bottom. It grounds me, it gives me a sense of stability I crave, a feeling that I am close to the earth down here. To the Mother.

I am returning.

The Indigo Girls sing "The Girl With the Weight of the World In Her Hands," and I fall face first into my two hands and cry. Here in this basement, surrounded by four lifetimes of memories and baggage, three thousand beautiful square feet above my head, it's too much. I should be happy, but I am not.

The weight of my responsibilities crushes me. My responsibility for my own happiness feels selfish, shallow, cruel, in fact. I have everything, why am I crying? Because I don't have everything. Everything has me.

"It's Beer O'Clock!" Wil yells from the bottom of the stairs, loud enough for me to hear all the way upstairs and down the hall. Another way I've tried to bring the best of Sisters to Portland is to stop what I'm doing, take a break at 5:00 and have a Corona with lime. It is perfect because Wil has discovered back-to-back episodes of "Seinfeld" from 5:00 – 6:00 PM. "Seinfeld" has been a strong thread that's knitted us together for years and now Wil loves it too.

Ed has a glass of cheap red wine in whatever glass or mug first grabs his eye. I have a Corona with the lime freshly scrubbed, sliced, squeezed then wedged expertly into the neck of the bottle. Wil has "chips" and calls this hour his "Chip O'Clock." During the commercials, Wil rises from his place on the wooden stool inches from the TV and tells jokes.

"Why did the dog cross the road?" he'll ask.

"To get to the other side?" I venture.

"No, Jerry, that's incorrect, Kramer, do you know?" Wil asks, assuming our appropriate names for our viewing of "Seinfeld."

"To catch a cat?" Ed will say.

"Yes! That is correct, Kramer! Good job, Kramer! George Costanza is proud of you, Kramer!"

Jane comes in and out to let us know she's around but seldom joins us for any length of time.

"Well, hello, Elaine!" Wil welcomes her each time she appears.

"Wil! You are *so* annoying," she says, eyes rolled to the heavens.

"Excuse me, Elaine, I am not Wil, I am George Costanza."

Usually that's enough to get her right back out of the room.

When Ed and I were dating and into our early marriage, we

faithfully watched "Seinfeld" each week. When we were new parents, the show had gone into syndication and came on each night at 7:00 PM. We'd get Jane fed, bathed and put down for the night and sit there together, done for the day, proud of our good job as parents. I'm thinking of this as Ed turns to me and says, "Remember when we thought parenting was easy? Remember when we sat and watched Seinfeld, all done for the night with time to ourselves? Didn't life seem easy then?"

I don't really have an easy answer to that seemingly easy question. No, it did not seem easy then. It should have, but it didn't. And that's what I'm struck with – we never know just how good we have it until we don't have it. Alone in Sisters, I was able to reconnect with myself as well as see just how good I actually have it – a gift, one I vow not to lose. I don't want to sit with Ed ten years from now and think the same thing, *Why didn't I appreciate what I had? Why didn't I bask in the glory of my beautiful, happy, healthy family? Why didn't I burst with gratitude?*

CHAPTER TWENTY-FOUR

I've been home a month now and I'm catching up with old friends I fell out of touch with over the summer. One of these friends is Val, a soul sister. In the time I've been gone, she's been continuing her training to become a Curandera, which is Spanish for "one who cures." That is Val, she is a cure for all that ails me.

In addition to her Curandera training, she's also begun practicing the art of animal readings, similar to Tarot or other types of readings, using cards that are symbolic. I've agreed to be a guinea pig, eager for time in her presence, eager for anything that gives me a map out of this maze that is my mind, eager for healing.

"Shuffle the cards until you feel they are ready," she says.

Eyes closed, I hold the deck in my hand offering up a small prayer to the Divine. "Please," I beg, "please show me the answers for which I seek." I hold the deck of fifty-two cards and shuffle in an intuitively-driven way until a nudge within says, "done."

She tells me to select one card at a time, place them on the table before us in a north, south, east, west formation, with a card in the center. I can have them face up or face down, whichever way feels right to me.

From the deck I "divine" which card to pick, which is what I say when I'm letting something greater than myself do the choosing. With one hand I hold the deck, now fanned before me and I wave the other over the top… trying to sense a vibe, a way of "knowing" which card is ready to tell me what to do, where to go, and who I am. In this manner I pull all five cards, placing them carefully in the way Val has instructed, north, south, east, west and center.

"First turn the north card over," she instructs. I turn the squirrel card over.

"The north represents the wisdom of the stars and our ancestors," she says. "Squirrels prepare for the future, they gather in times of plenty to save for times of scarcity. This is an instruction for you to clear your home, mind, and time from anything that is cluttering them. An untroubled heart and mind is where the gathered energy is stored."

This makes good sense. I watched the busy grey, long-tailed squirrels out the window in Sisters all summer. Busy little buggers, nervous and hyper. I find the fact that I've spent so much time recently doing just that, clearing and un-cluttering no accident.

"Now turn the card in the east position," Val says. I turn Salmon. "The east position represents new beginnings and enlightenment," she says. "You are like the salmon, swimming upstream, going against cultural norms and public opinion. Like the salmon, there is a point to all you do. You complete the life/death cycle. You will return to the point where you were born. You will do what you set out to do."

Of all the words in the world, "life/death cycle" hit me like a bullet.

"The card in the south position represents clarity and emotion," Val tells me. I turn over Frog. "Frog is associated with magic of both land and water. It is the totem of metamorphosis. It represents cleansing."

I just sit with that, I don't comment. This is all hitting me right between the eyes, and I don't have words yet to catch up with my thoughts. A metamorphosis is the perfect word for what I'm going through and have been going through. I thought I'd be done with this whole process this summer but I find myself mid-way, at best, since I've come back home.

"Now turn over the western card which symbolizes protection." I turn over Jaguar. "Jaguars devour the unclean aspects of human behavior. They don't falter with resolve to be their personal best at all times. They are impeccable and have integrity."

Wow. Another "no accident" moment. Impeccable and integrity, words I'm quite fond of and always in search of in others, but mostly myself. The word "devour" hits me funny though. In what ways do I "devour?" Immediately, I am reminded of all the ways I devour information from books, videos, the Internet, fellow journeyers, and this too, is a word that now deeply reverberates.

"Go on," I urge, still unable to speak, too impacted by all the bricks to the head.

"The last card, the center card, sums up all the lessons from the other four." I turn over Snake. "Ah, Snake," Val says. "We westerners have issues with snakes, but in most cultures they are revered, considered holy. Snakes have an acute sense of vibrations, they 'read' the situation intrinsically, intuitively. When they are done with their skin, their past, they shed it. Done. They represent birth, resurrection, initiation and wisdom."

"Does any of this ring true?" Val asks, big smile on her little pixie face.

"Every word. Every single word," I answer softly.

CHAPTER TWENTY-FIVE

The gong rings three times and I walk downstairs and take my seat at the prayer table. The Nag Champa incense smells lovely. It's a gray, dark morning and the light from the candles on the mantle and table bring a warming touch to the cold in my heart. Ed is there. His eyes light up when I enter. Jane smiles. Wil screws up his face to be funny. They are three of the most beautiful humans on the planet.

After prayer we scatter; Ed to work, the kids to school, and me to the shower. Today I have reason to get out of my pajamas. I am going to be trained in Reiki, a Japanese healing art I've been hearing a lot about and wanting to learn for some time. Val is putting together a group who want to be trained. She knows a Reiki master and through this master we will be attuned, his insight will pass through him to us. We will have working knowledge of this ancient laying on of hands. The timing couldn't be better. This is one of the bigger rocks in the grid I am psychically building to hold me.

I walk up to Val's cheerful blue house and press her heart-shaped doorbell. Val is there, beaming in her usual way. Behind her stands a man with the gentlest brown eyes I've ever seen in my life.

"Carrie," Val says, "this is Didier, the one I've been telling you about. He is the Reiki master."

I take hold of Didier's extended right hand but I want to grab hold of him in a hug and not let go. When he speaks, he is all French accent and twinkle. He smiles easily and I see the gold and silver in his mouth, teeth that are white and straight but not perfect. His curly brown shortly cut hair also holds strands of silver.

The day progresses and the wonders of Reiki are given to me in the attunement process. The other students and I move around and take turns practicing on each other. When it is my turn to lie down and be treated, Didier has my upper region. With hands on my eyes, ears, back of the head then throat, he blesses and heals me. When he comes to my heart chakra, the touch is almost too hot for comfort, it's as though I'm being burned by the sun. Eyes still closed, I reach up to move his hand gently away and am startled to realize his hands are nowhere near my heart -- they are in his lap, where they have been for several minutes now.

I realize I'm done. All the other practitioners are finished, just quietly waiting for me to open my eyes and join them back in the circle. When I do, we de-brief, talk about the experiences of both healer and patient. When I speak of my hot heart, I look over to Didier and he looks back with eyes of knowing, of pure love. Not a sexual love, but instead, a look that says to me, "I see you and you are amazing."

Tears well up in my eyes and I swallow rather than shed them. I've seen pure love from the eyes of my children and dearest of friends, the priest at the kids' school and a few other holy people. To see it from a "stranger" is powerful.

When the day is over and we are all gathering coats and shoes, I slip into the bathroom and look into the mirror. Eye to eye with myself, I look and say, "I see you and you are amazing."

CHAPTER TWENTY-SIX

It's finally spring here in Portland after one of the darkest, coldest, wettest winters in history. The lilacs, rhododendrons and azaleas are all in full bloom, nearly a month later than usual. March and April were months where every encounter with another Oregonian began with, "Aren't you sick of this weather? When is it ever going to be spring?" We all seem to have made the same agreement with the valley... we'll put up with all your rain, but we want to see that sun by April, at least. Now that it is May, we feel cheated out of a month of "our" spring, and are not happy about it.

Suddenly a commercial for Dairy Queen comes on, the volume grows louder, and the screen flashes with sights of waffle cone sundaes and Dilly Bars. My eyes turn from the window to the TV, and I say, "I'll take one of those, please!"

Soon after, I see Ed's car pulling into the driveway. Now that I think about it, it did get awfully quiet all of a sudden. I watch as Jane and Wil both pile out of the car with soft-served ice cream cones in their hands. Ed gets out of the car with a waffle cone sundae.

I go downstairs to open the front door for them, they're all smiles. "Here you go, Honey," Ed says, handing me the sundae.

"Thank you!" I say, "Did you get one for yourself?" I ask.

"No. I didn't want one, but you did."

I put the red spoon into the melting ice cream and walk with the three of them into the kitchen where we eat our ice cream and have some laughs.

I wasn't serious about wanting that sundae. I had forgotten I'd even said anything about it, but Ed is serious about showing me he loves me.

This is all I've ever wanted, what I have right here in this kitchen, right this minute: Laughter. Thoughtfulness. Kindness. Unconditional, pure love.

"I've got a crazy idea," Ed says to me one Sunday afternoon. "Let's take the kids and go to the pub for dinner!"

"That *is* a crazy idea," I say. We have been parents for fourteen years now and for almost twelve we've been the parents of a child with multiple special needs... where and what he will eat being a fundamental issue.

"No, think about it," Ed continues, "Wil can have a vanilla milkshake, you know he's been on a big vanilla milkshake kick, and we can all have burgers."

"Let me call the restaurant," I say before agreeing.

"Do you have vanilla milkshakes?" I ask when someone answers the phone.

"Yes, we do!" they assure me.

"Let's do it," I tell Ed.

When we tell Wil what we're planning he needs to know exactly what time we're leaving, exactly what time we'll return home, and if they will give him a spoon, not a straw, for him to use for his milkshake. Once all these bases have been covered, he's good to go.

"Jane!" I call up the stairs, "We're going to the pub for dinner. We're leaving in fifteen minutes!"

She comes running down the stairs, a confused look on her face.

"You and Daddy?"

"No, all four of us," I answer.

"All four of us?" she asks incredulously. The four of us have never, ever, not once been out to a restaurant together. Not even McDonald's.

We drive to the restaurant, park right in front and go in. Wil orders his vanilla milkshake. Ed orders a glass of house red wine. I order a Hefeweizen. Jane requests a root beer and we sit there, just the four of us, together at a table.

My eyes look from person to person, husband, daughter, son and back around again. Could this be the same family who has tried unsuccessfully to sit down for a meal together year after year? Are we the same four people who have so many food, noise, light, and smell sensitivities that we cannot accept invitations to other people's homes for dinner? Is this the same group of people who buys the same exact things from the grocery store week after week because we don't like to try new things? Is this us?

I raise my glass and say to Ed, "Even if a fire breaks out and we all run screaming from this building in five minutes, I'm going to go ahead and declare this a huge victory."

Ed raises his glass and clinks it to mine. He looks me in the eye and says, "To us."

The next day, I've got one foot catching the dishwasher door as it falls open, one arm reaching under the sink to grab the detergent, Wil at the counter eating sourdough toast, Jane next to him waiting to have her hair French braided before school.

Ever since my sabbatical at Sisters, Ed has taken the morning duty four out of five days. I do Wednesday, our late start day. Ed has started going up to the church associated with our Catholic school. He slides in through the back door, sits until Mass is almost over then leaves. He does not go there to socialize. He does not go there with his thinking mind to decide if organized religion is a joke. He goes there to see how it feels to sit amongst the holy elders and be still.

Compromise is a strange thing, by definition you give a little, get a little. If you're lucky, you give a little and get a lot. I am lucky. My giving has come in terms of what I've stopped doing, not what I've had to actually give, the only giving is up. No one could have ever convinced me of this before, but the more control and martyrdom I've given up the more I've received.

Before Ed left I said, "Hey! Your birthday is coming up, what do you want to do?"

"You know what I'd really, really like?" he answered, "I'd like us all to go to Sisters together for Memorial Weekend. Are you up for that?"

The four of us have not been together at the house in Sisters for two years. It has become my sanctuary away from them. I know he knows this. I know his question is, "Are you ready to share your sanctuary? Have we loved you enough that you don't need to get away from us?"

"OK," I answer.

"Really?" he says, eyes holding back tears.

"Really," I say.

I was in Sisters alone almost a year ago. Wow. Feels so much longer than that. I'm not even close to the same woman that left this house then.

I spend the morning researching labyrinths. Val's sister-in-law lives in Sisters and has one on her property. I make plans to go take a look Memorial Weekend. I've got some new ideas for those old rocks. The grid that I placed there a year ago did what it was supposed to, it harnessed energy from the land and worked to heal me. It feels important that my whole family help me pick them up now and replace them along the ground in a new pattern.

According to Clement Jewitt, "Each man's life is a labyrinth at the center of which lies his own death, and even after death it may be that he passes through a final maze before it is all ended for him. Within the great maze of a man's life are many smaller ones, each seemingly complete in itself, and in passing through each one he dies in part, for in each he leaves behind him a part of his life and it lies dead behind him. It is a paradox of the labyrinth that the center appears to be the way to freedom."

CHAPTER TWENTY-SEVEN

Wil comes to find me and says, "OK, Mom, I'm going to ask you a question, and you have three choices for answers. You can say, 'Sure!' or you can say, 'Maybe,' but you cannot say, 'No.'"

Not bothering to explain that is not really three choices, I agree to hear the question.

"Can you go to Safeway and buy a bottle of Aquafina?"

"Right now?" I ask, looking at my watch and planning my "out."

"Yes! Right now! You will go to Safeway and you will buy me one bottle of Aquafina. You will open up that thing they have like a refrigerator? The one you just walk right up to and open? The one you just open up the door and take the Aquafina?" His eyes bounce with joy just talking about the refrigerator containing bottles and bottles of expensive and environmentally disastrous water bottles.

"Oh, I don't know, Wil, we have two cases of water in the garage that you've already talked me into buying."

"Mom! That is not one of the answers! You are supposed to *think about it before you answer it!*" a line obviously borrowed from his teacher.

"OK, I will think about it."

"Great!" he beams, bouncing off as if I just handed him a winning lottery ticket.

I go back to writing and forget all about the Aquafina.

For a full two minutes.

"Mom," he bounces back in, "did you have time to think about going to Safeway? Before you decide, Daddy says you can either take Jane to Youth Group, or you can go to Safeway, we need bread."

I quickly save my work and trudge downstairs.

"I will take Jane to Youth Group and on the way home I

will get the Aquafina and bread from Safeway!" I announce to the gathered family, smiling proudly at myself for killing three birds with one stone and giving an evil thought as to how I can work this in my favor later.

I do just that, and when I return triumphant, I am met at the door by a very sad and deeply troubled, young boy.

"I was scared to death! You did not take me to Safeway! I wanted to *go* with you to Safeway! You were supposed to *take* me to Safeway, not buy Aquafina without me! I do not want that stupid Aquafina! That is a *bad* bottle of Aquafina! I am so sad you did not take me to Safeway! Why did you not take me to Safeway? Why did you scare me to death?"

He cannot catch all the tears pouring from his eyes, both sleeves and two Kleenex are not enough for the spillage. He is hardly intelligible through all the sobbing. His little heart is broken - fully broken. He is holding the Sharpie pen in his hand, all ready to write his name on the bottle of Aquafina that he wanted to choose from the special refrigerator, and I've gone and blown his plan.

"I am so sorry, Wil, so sorry! I didn't understand! I thought I was supposed to bring it back for you!"

"No! That was *not* what you were supposed to do! You did not follow directions!"

I quickly determine that this is one of those times when I must give in, buckle, turn things around at all cost, or it will escalate to the point of no return, and frankly, I'm just not up for that scene tonight.

"OK, get your shoes and coat on, let's go."

One last wipe down of his face and he's pulled himself together enough to get in the car.

Still snuffling, recovering from the aftershocks of sobbing, he says, "Were you trying to deal me a chimp?"

"Beg pardon?" I ask, eyes on the rainy windshield, mind a million miles away.

"You were trying to deal a chimp to me, weren't you, Mom!"

"Excuse me?" I ask, now fully intrigued with what he is

saying with my mind frantically searching for the real meaning. "Ahhh..." I say, as it slowly dawns on me, "No, I don't think I'm dealing *with* a chimp, Wil. I'm sorry about the mix-up."

"That's OK, Mom, I won't deal a chimp to you either."

When we took Wil to visit Santa a few weeks ago, Wil sat on his lap and looked bewildered when Santa asked, "What do you want for Christmas?" Wil, fully believing in Santa at age eleven but not fully believing in the whole "wanting" thing answered, "You tell me."

"How about a train?" Santa suggested desperately.

"Yes! That is a great idea, Santa! Yes! I want a train!" Wil exuded.

Hopping off Santa's lap he comes rushing over to me, "Mom! I am going to get a train from Santa!"

The boy has never shown an interest in trains. We've had train videos. We've had trains, trains and more trains at our house. Not one bit of interest. I finally packed them all up and gave them away. Years ago.

Ed decides to spiff up his old train set from childhood, still in a box in his parents' basement. I wrap it in special-just-from-Santa paper and put it out on Christmas Eve.

Wil wakes at 6:00 jumping up and down and says, "I want to go see my train! Where the hell is my train? Is that my damn train?" he asks, pointing to the box lying beside his bursting-with-gifts stocking.

Pulling the wrapping off so fast it all but ignites, he sees the train, grabs it, hugs it, dances, swears, yells, jumps and is thrilled for the rest of the day. He doesn't actually play with it for more than five minutes, but is thrilled.

He had fun opening his brand new Nintendo DS Lite and several hundred dollars worth of other "things" but the train, ah, the train.

As he brushed his teeth he says through his foamy mouth, "This is the best Christmas I ever had."

"I'm so glad," I respond. "What were the two best things about it?"

"The train!" he answers.

"Yes, that was such a great gift from Santa. What else was great about Christmas?" I probe.

"You were there!" he answers.

"Mom," Wil asks Friday morning before school, "are you excited it is the weekend? Are you excited that you can watch me play my games all weekend long?"

"Uh huh," I answer mindlessly.

"Because I have a lot of games this weekend, and you get to watch them all! I have NBA, NFL, SEC and Pac 10! I have high school games, too and I have some all-star games! Aren't you excited to watch me play all my games all weekend long?"

"Uh huh," I think I answer, not really sure, still in full denial that we already have a weekend after just two and a half days back to school.

First thing when he gets home Friday, "Mom, I have a game at 4:00, another one at 6:00 and another one at 7:30 tonight. Aren't you excited to watch those three games?"

A familiar tightness in my neck begins to emerge. I try to massage it away even though I know it won't really go away until 8:00 AM Monday when I see the back of him walking down the street to school.

"OK, so it's time to get ready for my 4:00 game. It is the Golden State Warriors and Boston College Eagles. Don't forget. Who do you want to win? Boston College? The Eagles? Are you going to cheer for the Eagles? Are they your favorite? Are you a fan of the Eagles? Because I am a fan of the Eagles, and I want the Eagles to win. They are going to win thirty-five to twenty-eight."

I walk down the steps to my basement as though I'm headed to the gallows. I systematically turn on all the right lamps; neither of us can stand the harsh glare of the overhead lights, and situate myself in the center of the futon. I place

Elmo, the mascot for the Eagles on my left, and Sam, the pink Build-a-Bear and mascot for the Warriors, on my right. They are the cheerleaders and when their teams score I am to raise the appropriate mascot in wild excitement and shout, "Good job!" to their team. In their voices.

On my lap is the "score board." It is a small, nine by eleven inch white board. Strict rules dictate that I am to write the names of the team on the top, mark the score as zero to start with and then as he "announces" the teams, I am to take note on the proper side of the board. Elmo and Sam must be extremely enthusiastic. In their voices.

We've got your Taylor Wilcox, Tyler Wilcox, Jordan McWhoo-ha and Michael, whose last name is whatever day of the week it happens to be. Elmo and Sam really love these names, and say so, repeatedly. In their voices.

There is no rhyme or reason to the number of "halves" the game can have. Three is quite common. The game may or may not have halves of equal length. Overtimes occur frequently. Booth reviews, time-outs and slow motion all have been known to slow the game considerably. A typical game lasts 30 minutes and leaves me writhing in agony and Wil smiling ear-to-ear. The more miserable I am, the happier he is.

Saturday we had games at 9:00, 11:00, 1:00, 3:00, 5:00 and 7:00. We also had scheduled trips to Safeway for bottles of water.

Today we've had games at 9:00, 11:00, 1:00, 3:00, 4:30 and two more coming up. We've been to Safeway today, too. Twice.

It's now Sunday at 5:47 and there's another game at 6:00 followed by the last game of the weekend at 7:30 tonight. At eight, Sam, Elmo and I will tuck Wil into bed. Sam and Elmo will stay with him. As I close his door and begin to feel myself sigh deeply, his last words will be, "Thanks, Mom for watching all my games this weekend. We really had fun, didn't we? Aren't you excited for my games after school tomorrow? There's a game at 4:00, 6:00 and 7:30! Who do you want to win? Do you want the Eagles? Are you an Eagles fan?"

This is what I "got" for Mother's Day from Wil - the use of Elmo, Sam and Lucky for ninety minutes. Elmo was wrapped in newspaper, Sam and Lucky in kitchen towels. He wrapped them up the night before, which means he chose my happiness over his; he didn't sleep with this tremendous trio.

In the morning he was beside himself waiting for his sister to wake up so they could surprise me. He presented me with the three bundles and jumped up and down the whole time (three seconds) that it took me to open them.

"Look! It's Elmokins! I am giving you my brother! Little Elmokins! Do you love him? Do you love Elmokins? Do you love my little brother???"

"Yes! I LOVE him! Thank you so much!"

"You get to have him until 9:00 AM. Are you excited to have him until 9:00 AM?"

"Yes! Thank you!"

"And Sam! I am giving you Sam! Do you love Sam? Do you love my brother, Sam?"

"I love Sam, too."

"You get to have Sam until 9:00, too. And Lucky! You get to have Luckykins until 9:00, too! Are you excited to have my brother, Luckykins, until 9:00???"

"Yes! I am *thrilled*!"

Picking up all three of his favorite brothers, giving them each a full mouth kiss, hug and a twirl, he says, "Happy Mother's Day, Mom!"

It was.

Wil is in the bathtub tonight, and we're trying to get him to do the whole bathing process himself.

He calls me in, "Mom! I'm done! I washed my body! I washed my hair!" And sure enough, he's fully lathered when I get there.

"OK, we need to rinse you off with clean water," I say,

grabbing the small pail and turning on the tap.

"Please let me do it? Please let me pour water on my own head!"

"OK," I say, handing him the first filled bucket.

"Wait. I'm not ready. I need to pray."

Eyes lowered, head bowed, he says, "Dear Lord, please make the water not hot. Please make the water not hot. Please make the water not hot." Then, crossing himself he says, "In the name of the Father, Son and Holy Spirit, amen."

He grabs the bucket from my hands, dumps it on his head and says, "My prayers have been answered!"

"Do you want to go to the park and count drinking fountains, Mom?" Wil asks twice a day.

And twice a day we drive to the park, the one that sprawls at least a mile long, and many football fields deep. We walk the ground together and count the drinking fountains. We've found six. Wil is convinced there are seven and if we just look hard enough we'll find that last one.

His almost twelve-year-old hand in mine is almost as big. Where once he reached up and I reached down, we are nearly shoulder-to-shoulder, eye-to-eye as we walk hand in hand.

Is it habit, I wonder, that has him reaching for my hand and holding it awkwardly, still not sure how one fits within another in a comfortable way?

Is it affection?

Is it the need to steady his awkward gait on the uneven grass?

Is it purely spontaneous, no thought whatsoever, just the purity of a child responding out of love without ego?

I hold his hand and listen to him talk about the fountains.

"There is one hiding in the trees, Mom," he says.

"One by the tennis courts."

"One by the baseball field."

"One is on the other side of a fence, but Daddy lifts me over and I get a drink. You don't have to lift me over, but we need to go see it anyway. That is number four."

"Number five is by the bathrooms."

"Number six is by the white pick-up truck that works here."

"I know there is a number seven, though," he says every time.

He's probably right. One thing I know for sure is when we find it we'll be together holding hands.

"Mom, how many friends did I have over after school today?" Wil asks, milk dribbling down his chin, Fruity Pebbles being shoved in his mouth, eyes turned towards me.

"You had four friends over," I answer.

"But there were six people," he argues.

"Matthew, Michael, Greg and Ian, four friends," I argue back, "plus you. Five people all together."

"And Ian!" he says.

"Yes. Ian. Michael. Greg. Matthew. Four."

"And Matthew!" he says.

I sigh. Heavily.

"MATTHEW, IAN, GREG AND MICHAEL!" I shout.

"And Michael!" he says, dimples in full swing.

"I said Michael!" I say, "you're killing me here!"

I fling myself dramatically on the window seat, pretend to gasp for breath, arms flailing around. He nearly chokes on the Fruity Pebbles, such is his joy.

When I stop he looks at me, smiles and says, "Mom? Let's go back to the killing."

CHAPTER TWENTY-EIGHT

We spent yesterday in Seaside, Oregon, one and a half hours away from Portland. The weather was a perfect sixty-two degrees, sunny, clear blue sky, and best of all, we followed Wil's month-long plan for the exact execution of the day.

"We will leave at 10:55 AM and get to the beach at 12:25 PM. Then we will go to "the claw" at the arcade and you will grab a football for me. Then we will go to the sand and I will play CFL (Canadian Football League) for three games. And you will keep score. You will write in the sand. Don't forget. Promise you won't forget. You will watch three CFL games and you will not forget to keep score."

We left at 10:55, arrived at the arcade, where I promptly turned a twenty dollar bill into eighty quarters, and inserted at least forty of them into a hungry claw machine until I successfully grabbed the four inch New England Patriots stuffed football (retail value? .99).

Delighted, we then proceeded to the beach where Ed was first instructed to create a "tee" for Wil to kick off. Donning the hockey-turned-football helmet we brought from home, calculator in his right hand, ten dollar football in his left, the game commenced.

"Are you remembering to keep score? Remember, it is CFL. Don't forget to keep score. Promise you won't forget to keep score?"

I kept score.

I didn't forget.

We rented two sand bikes and Ed, Jane and I took turns on them, spelling each other from Wil, who we renamed "The Barker" as he barked orders non-stop.

"I'll go on a bike ride with you, Jane, Daddy can stay with The Barker."

Wil beams - loves being The Barker - loves that we are all

about to lose it with him, but never actually do because just when he's pushed us to the limit, he says or does something so funny, so endearing, we all laugh.

"Dad! Will you build me a sand TV? Will you build me a sand chair to watch my sand TV? Will you find me a stick remote to use on my sand TV?"

Ed follows The Barker's instructions perfectly and for a full ninety seconds Wil is enthralled with his sand system, just long enough for me to get a photo showing his legs splayed in perfect recliner fashion, eyes fixed straight ahead at the "TV" and the "remote" poised straight at it, clicking it to channel 55, for "Seinfeld."

"Dad! I am watching George Costanza losing it! He is saying 'jack ass!'"

Jane and I move our beach blankets away from the boys and try to read our books but The Barker won't hear of it.

"It is time for salt water taffy! We will get a twenty-pack! We will leave in five minutes and we will get salt water taffy and you will pick out 20 pieces for me because I really need a twenty-pack!"

We'd been warned that he would need saltwater taffy at 4:30 and at 4:25 he gave us our marching orders.

As we walk down to the candy store he grabs my hand, holds it while simultaneously trying to break free and clutching tightly.

"I like holding your hand, Barker," I say, "but I can't tell if you want to hold it or let go?"

That's it, isn't it? He's getting older, twelve now, and he can't decide either, which side of childhood he is on.

I went to Safeway yesterday, and hadn't been there in over a week. It had changed. Significantly. It's been in the process of a major remodel, but in the week I was absent the entrance moved, the carts are in a different place, the little post office inside is on the other side now, and they added a Starbucks! I go grocery shopping at peak older population times, so it was the little old ladies and me. They were not happy.

"Miss! Can you help me find _____" I heard many times.

"Crap!" one particularly spicy older woman said, "I'm so damn tired of them moving everything! I can't find anything!"

People were complaining to their shopping partners, they were complaining to the Safeway employees and many were complaining to themselves, (or God?) out loud.

Change is hard and yet inevitable. Just when we get used to the "new," it changes again. Every time. And maybe it's easier to complain about the changes at our local grocery store than to deal with the changes in our personal lives, or bodies, or families, or, or, or...

Or maybe, the complaints of not being able to find anything, are just that, no hidden meanings, no deeper truths, simply people wanting to know where things are.

When I get going on my "I hate change" tirades, I try to remember how many "Why don't things ever change?" tirades I've had. When Wil took "forever" to move out of the toddler phase, took "forever" to be potty trained, took "forever" to be left to his own devices safely for more than two seconds, I prayed up a storm that this would all change. And eventually it did.

And you know what that boy did yesterday? That twelve-year-old rode a bicycle with no training wheels... just him and his developing balance and a bike.

That's change.

That's big change.

Maybe today I'll ride with him up to Safeway.

Jane is playing on the freshman volleyball team and having a ball but nobody is more excited than Wil.

As soon as teams were made and schedules given, a clipboard got passed around asking the parents to sign up for a few shifts at the "Snack Shack," as a fundraiser for the sport teams whereby many bags of popcorn and slices of pizza change hands.

Oh, and water bottles.

And candy.

"Mom! I will help you at the Snack Shack! I will help you sell water bottles and candy! You will tell me what the people order and I will just RUN and get it and hand it to the people! I will just run and get them their candy and run and get them their water bottle. You will just tell me and I will do all the running!"

That was in August.

Every day since then, it's been a steady stream of, "Mom! Only _____ more days until we work the Snack Shack! You will just tell me what the people want and I will just RUN to get it! The people will say, 'I'll have a water bottle, please,' and you will tell me, 'Wil! One water bottle, please,' and I will just run and go get it and then I'll hand it to the person and I will say, 'Here is your water bottle!'"

Tuesday is Snack Shack day and Jane had been home sick Monday so Wil got worried.

"Mom. We will still work at the Snack Shack even if Jane is too sick to go to school, right? Even if she is not playing volleyball we will still sell water bottles and candy at the Snack Shack, right?"

Tuesday morning and Jane was still too sick to go to school. Again, I raised my right hand and placed it on the Bible and swore the Snack Shack plan was still in effect.

Tuesday afternoon I picked him up from school, and he's not even fully in the car, door still wide open, backpack flung on the floor and he starts in, "Mom. You did not forget the Snack Shack, did you? What time will we go to the Snack Shack tonight? What time will I sell the water bottles and candy?"

I assured him we were all systems go for the Snack Shack and we would leave at 4:15, watch the end of Jane's team's game, then be right on time to start peddling at 5:00, as planned.

"Let's go over this one more time," he says, all business,

once back at home. "In fact, let me write you a script so you can study your lines. Then you will put the script in your purse and have it at the Snack Shack just in case you forget. But you will not forget, right? You promise not to forget?"

He digs out paper and pencil and writes me the "script," "OPEN REVERFARTER FOR WATER" and "OPEN DRAWER FOR CANDY."

"Do you understand your job? Do you understand that you will open the refrigerator for water and hand me the water and I will run and take it to the person? Do you understand that if the person wants candy, you will open the drawer and I will just give it right to the person, just like that? Do you understand? Do we need to go over this one more time?"

After many more promises that I would deliver on my end of the bargain, we headed on over to the Snack Shack.

He worked up a sweat with all the running back and forth and endeared himself to most of the student body, many parents and the principal.

When our one-hour shift ended he was reluctant to leave, just sure he'd left shoes too big to fill. Anyone can hand out candy and water bottles, not just anyone can do so with such unadulterated joy.

Wil has two friends in the backyard with him right now. I've got all the windows open so I can hear their conversations which is proving entertaining, delightful, and heartening.

These two boys are relatively new in Wil's life. One just came to his school last year, the other is new this year. Each year that Wil gets older and new people join the fold, we hold our breath hoping the culture of acceptance that surrounds him will withstand the new influences.

Last year, four new boys moved into the class that'd been together since kindergarten. Those four new boys quickly wormed their way into Wil's heart, and he, theirs.

This year, sixth grade, three new boys were added to the mix. It's only October first, and check, check, check, all three are in, in, in.

Wil's out there telling them, "We're not going to use bad words anymore. We're going to just say 'blank,' instead. Like instead of saying poop stain, we're going to say blank stain. Get it? You try it."

They get it.

They're out there saying blank more times than Carter's got pills.

One "slipped."

"I guess you forgot," Wil gently reminds, "we aren't saying bad words. We're saying 'blank,' instead."

The kid says, "I didn't forget! I didn't say a bad word!"

"You said, 'dumb,' dumb is a bad word. Don't be a blank. Don't say a bad word like dumb. Promise you won't be a blank. Promise you won't say bad words like that anymore."

They promised.

I promise not to forget.

Wil and I were doing our usual Wednesday TV night thing and watching a show where the family is flying to Hawaii. Wil asks, "Have I ever been on an airplane?"

"Yes. You've been on two. Remember when we went to Disneyland when you were in first grade?"

He nods.

"And when you were a tiny baby I took you to New York to visit my friend Terry."

"I don't remember that," he says.

I nod, while remembering the hell that was that trip. I was out of my mind the whole time with his crying. Picking up on my thoughts, he says, "Did I cry a lot?"

"Yes, yes you did. Did you know that you used to cry a lot when you were a baby?"

This is the first time he and I have ever discussed this.

He nods.

"Do you remember *why* you used to cry?" I ask, hoping the Wise One will enlighten me.

"Some babies just do," he says.

And I am one shade lighter.

I put Wil to bed. I've completed the full battery of bedtime routines and am heading down the hall to my own bedroom. I pass the two opposing doors that separate our rooms and I think... *That's the space I hold, right there in the middle. I am seated on the hardwood floor right between two doors, feet shoved hard against one, pushing, pushing, pushing, and back against the other, holding back, holding back, holding back. All I need to do to stop this insanity is just stand up. That's it. Just. Stand. Up.*

I keep walking to my room, full of myself for my deep and powerful insight when Wil pulls me back into the moment.

"Mom," he calls from the opposite side of his door, "What time do you think you'll wake up tomorrow?"

"I think I'll wake up at 5:30 tomorrow. What time do you think you'll wake up?" I ask.

I think I'll wake up at 6:10," he says.

"Okay. See you at 6:10," I say, "I love you, goodnight."

Back to my reverie and he cuts in again.

"Mom! Are you going to jump up and down?"

"Excuse me?" I ask, not knowing what he's talking about because I'm all about doors now and have long lost the magic of my moment with him.

"When you wake up at 5:30? Are you going to jump up and down because you will be so excited to wake up?"

"Oh. Good idea. Yes, I will jump up and down at 5:30," I answer.

"Don't forget!" he says. "Don't forget to be excited when you wake up tomorrow. Promise you won't forget."

"Okay. I promise not to forget," I say before making the final steps to my room, leaving that door open and vowing to leave all other doors open, too.

CHAPTER TWENTY-NINE

We went to see Santa yesterday after school - Ed and I figure this is our fifteenth time, and perhaps the last.

Jane was a good sport. We didn't make her tell Santa what she wants for Christmas but we did make her pose for a picture - some traditions just aren't going to be broken no matter how old you are - sorry.

Wil loved every minute of the experience. He talked to Santa for a long time, but then when he got up to leave he realized he'd forgotten to tell Santa what he wanted. Santa could see his internal struggle, got up off his chair and followed Wil all the way over to us, patiently nodding and listening as Wil struggled to get the words out of his brain and into the loving ears of Santa.

Eventually the words came out, "I... want... you... know... it's black...it's pretend... it's small..., it has tape on it...Mr. G. puts it on the chalkboard...it's a BEETLE!"

Santa winked at me and said, "Okay, Santa will take care of that but Santa is also going to bring you special things he's picked out *just* for you."

Wil beamed, looked up at Santa and said, "Oh! That would be great! Thanks!"

Earlier in the day Wil's aide Jenn had Wil do his grammar work on the computer and they tied it to Christmas:

Christmas Presents by Wil

I like Christmas because every 12 months is Christmas Eve and Christmas day. Presentes are fun to open. What I want for christmas is a fake black beetle with tape on it And playtao and new white board markers and books and candy. That's what I realy want. I will open in it on the 24th.

Ed and I went Christmas shopping and left Jane with Wil. When we returned, Wil was in front of his computer fully engrossed in Googling something. He's an excellent speller, and can maneuver Google like you wouldn't believe. He's so fast and so accurate it makes me dizzy to watch, so I don't. I just occasionally peer over his head to make sure he hasn't stumbled on anything inappropriate. He did find a bleeped out version of Sesame Street's The Count, but that's not so much inappropriate as just plain funny.

Anyway. All this is leading to the fact that by the time I got home and took a peek at what he'd been Googling... it was "blue water bottles with black tops."

For over an hour.

He has a red water bottle with a black top and he'd really like a blue one, too. You know, for trading off when the red one is dirty. His teacher wants the kids to bring eco-friendly reusable water bottles to school rather than the recyclable ones you use and "toss." Sometimes "Red" is dirty, and this can make for a rough morning.

He didn't grow impatient. He didn't grow tired. With dogged perseverance he just kept putting different key words into Google to try to find what he was looking for.

Finally, I grew both tired and impatient after only five minutes of watching from the sidelines. I got up closer, looked at his most recent Google search, and he had typed, "BLUE WATER BOTTLE LIKE THE ONE I HAVE."

He thinks Google *knows* him.

And his water bottle.

And what he means.

And who am I to second guess the boy?

Maybe Google does.

I recently had coffee with a friend and as we got our cups and looked around for a place to sit, I intentionally steered her towards one corner, away from a table where four grown men were seated. But it was a small cafe and I could still easily overhear the four men's' conversation, no matter how hard I tried not to.

One of the men had developmental disabilities and the other three could not have been kinder towards him.

It broke my heart.

They asked how he'd done during the recent snowstorm that stranded people for days/weeks.

"Okay," he answered.

"What did you do all that time?" one asked.

"TV. Lots of TV," he answered.

"Anyone check on you?" another asked.

"My sister. My sister called every night. My sister calls *every* night."

One of the men at the table had watched me as I looked for a place to sit. He'd seen me look at them, notice the man with the developmental differences and subsequently choose another table. A more distant one.

Throughout my conversation with my friend I saw the man look up at me and catch my eye.

In his eyes I saw the question, "Why do you avoid us? Don't you understand?"

I avoided them because I do. All too well. I couldn't bear to let my mind go to a distant day when Ed and I are gone and Wil lives all alone just watching TV all day.

And where his sister calls at night.

Every night.

Because she will.

I know she will.

That day, for me, is all too close to home.

Jenn, sent me an e-mail today with the subject line, "Get a load of this!"

> *Carrie,*
> *This is the best so far. It was supposed to involve the wild animals that they have been researching. The ad was to look for help in the area of where their animal*

lives. Anyway, that was too much for Wil, so he was to create a help wanted ad to find someone to assist Wil with his job. He chose his job and then began writing the ad. His instructions were to describe what kind of work they would be doing and when. He also had to include what type of characteristics the person should have in order to get the job.
ENJOY!
Jenn

Wil
1-13-2009

HELP WANTED

I'm looking for a grabge man helper for me. Monday though Saturday from 8:25 to 12:30 is when I need help. When I'm 20 years old that's when all be needing help. I will be the driver you will be the dumper. You will be the gabage can picker upper. I will pay you five doallers. I need a person who will be be good be nice and be in a good mood. And don't forget.

Last night I put Wil to bed and I said, "I really liked your Help Wanted ad! Good job!"

He said, "Yea, I'm probably not going to need to hire anyone though because my sons are going to do the job. My sons Ted and Brandon. I'm going to have five sons. You will have to be the nanny for the three youngest boys, Cameron, Taylor and Mikey. I will take Ted and Brandon with me. Ted will be the picker upper, Brandon will be the dumper."

"That sounds really great," I said. "Jenn was really proud of how well you did on that assignment. Did you tell her about all the sons?"

Not answering that question he said, "That Jenn, she threw

a T-bomb at me!"

"A T-bomb?" I asked, wondering if the T-bomb was anything like an F-bomb and if throwing one was anything like dropping one … not being able to fathom Jenn throwing, dropping or in any way tossing obscenities at my son at school.

"Yea! She said we had to use the white board on Thursday when we do math and we have to show our work. Then we have to erase it for the next person!"

"So how'd she throw a T-bomb?" I asked.

"She said we had to do that on THURSDAY!"

That Jenn. I need to speak with her. How dare she use the days of the week when speaking to *my* son!

I'm in the laundry room moving load number three from washer to dryer, and I hear it: clink, clink, clink. Something has fallen from someone's pocket, and is banging around in there but I can't see it.

I unload and shake each article of clothing: jeans, hoodies, towels, uniform pants, still can't find it.

Clink, clink, clink.

The last piece is out, safely loaded in the dryer, and I dig my hand and half my arm in there and swipe away.

Finally, my fingers land on something rough on one side, smooth on the other and very tiny.

A tooth.

Wil's tooth.

I go into the living room, interrupt his viewing of "The Yelling Show," which is what he calls John Hagen's "Praise the Lord," and ask, "Did you lose a tooth?"

"It's a long story," he answers me without even looking up.

"*When* did you lose a tooth?"

"It's a long story," he repeats.

"Okay, so don't tell me the long story, just answer yes or no. Were you at school when a tooth fell out and you just shoved it in your pocket?"

"I told you, it's a long story," he says, slightly miffed but still refusing to take his eyes off John Hagen.

I go find Ed.

"Classic!" I say, showing him the tooth, "Look what I found in the dryer!"

"Is that a *tooth?*" he says.

"No, not *a* tooth, *the* tooth. The tooth I've taken him to a dentist and an orthodontist over. The one that wouldn't come out when the big one started coming in right on top. The one we've been watching to see if it needs to be pulled. The one I've been driving him all over the city for. The tooth that has kept me up at night because I couldn't imagine how we'd ever deal with him having to get a tooth pulled. *That* tooth."

"That's about right," Ed says.

CHAPTER THIRTY

In Oregon, we have a very cool thing called Outdoor School. For one week, sixth graders get a week-long field trip with their teacher, adults and high school counselors, and a life-changing experience.

Outdoor School is not new, both Ed and I went when we were in sixth grade and for thousands of kids it's their favorite week of their entire grade school experience.

Sleeping bags, bunk beds, campfire, songs, communal meals, occasional showers, and some big time bonding are all highlights of Outdoor School. For those kids who fidget and endure year after year of sitting at a desk, for one week they are free, free, gloriously free.

For some kids, this week away is full of firsts - first sleepover, first time away from home, first camping trip, first taste of well-supervised independence.

For some kids, therapy is required in advance to prepare the child for all those firsts hitting at the same time.

For other kids, everything is taken in stride and parents simply drop them off at the bus stop on Sunday and pick them back up on Friday.

And then there's Wil.

Outdoor School has been very accommodating in meeting the needs of thousands of special needs students through the years, but those are *other* people's children. Not mine.

In his twelve plus years of life Wil has never slept anywhere other than our house or a grandparent's house.

He doesn't shower, he bathes with a lot of help in about three inches of water.

He doesn't eat "regular" food, at regular times. Right now, he pretty much only eats Cinnamon Toast Crunch Cereal at 5:00 AM and 5:00 PM. That might actually work, since who can't be talked into pouring him a bowl of cereal and splashing on some milk? But Outdoor School isn't until April and by then he could be back on garlic toast which is labor-intensive and very, very stinky.

He has certain TV shows, which watching are imperative to his state of well-being. "Nanny 911" on Tuesdays at 4:00 - we nearly get a speeding ticket each week making it back from getting Jane in time for that one. And what about "Drake & Josh," "Praise the Lord," and "iCarly?" Huh? What about those? Do they show *those* at Outdoor School? No. I don't think so.

So clearly, this won't work.

But each day he comes home a little more excited about Outdoor School, with a little bit more information and a little bit more buy in.

And each day my heart breaks a little bit more.

My greatest fear has always been that he will never live independently.

Now it's that he might.

Ash Wednesday has come and gone and Wil survived. Each year he sweats it (and crosses it off on the calendar) because he is fundamentally opposed to the "rule" (not sure if it's global or just at his school) that says you cannot say "alleluia" during Lent. Wil likes to say alleluia. He likes it a lot. I could take this one on but I chose not to.

He went to school and then went to Mass at 11:00 on a Wednesday when everyone knows Mass is at 8:20 on Thursdays. Period.

He also went up for the marking of the ash cross on his forehead and didn't wipe it off on his long-sleeved, white uniform shirt two seconds later.

Then he came home and let out a string of alleluias that had been pent up like firecrackers ready to explode. "Mom, I am going to watch 'Family Guy' and listen to all the bad words, and I am going to say 'alleluia,' and I am going to say all the bad words they say on 'Family Guy' except 'stupid' and 'idiot' because I do not like those bad words."

As he's talking and wildly gesticulating, my eyes are fixed on that black cross on his forehead.

His astrological natal chart forms a cardinal cross.

He is my savior - this boy has saved me from myself. He personifies St. Francis' message, "Preach the gospel at all times, if necessary use words." Before he was born, I was more concerned about a clean house than a clean heart. I was more caught up in what others thought of me, why they thought it and how I could control all that. I was worried about being like everyone else. Now, I have been freed from being anything but myself and he has forced me to celebrate all that he is, to see his differences as gifts, not disabilities.

Eckhart Tolle eloquently talks about the symbolism of the Christian cross. He says the horizontal line represents this lifetime with a clear beginning and ending, birth to death. The vertical line is the unending line; our soul, which is eternal.

Wil lives perfectly where those two lines intersect: the now. His soul and horizontal life are always in alignment.

Always.

Alleluia.

CHAPTER THIRTY-ONE

Five years ago, when Wil was seven turning eight, we drew up a standard will, dividing everything down the middle for our two kids. "I recommend you give them their money in chunks, at pre-determined times," the attorney said. "For instance, a chunk upon graduating from college or age twenty-five, whichever comes first. Then another chunk at age thirty, and maybe a third chunk at forty. It serves as both an incentive for going to college, staying in college and protects them, too. That way they don't get all their money at once and they have more coming to them as they work and mature."

We are all about incentives and protection. We created and signed those wills, put them in a safe place and forgot all about them until the attorney just called to remind us it'd been five years since we did them, and perhaps we should review them – make changes.

"We have been told we need a special needs trust," I tell the attorney when he calls, "for our son."

"I wasn't aware of his needs," he says. "Yes, let's meet to set that up and to change your will to provide for his long-term care."

I hang up the phone, look at my watch, it's 4:45 PM. Ed will be home soon, but it's time for Beer O'Clock right now. I grab a Corona from the fridge, slice off a piece of lime, squeeze it, slip it into the neck of the bottle and plop down on the couch. I close my eyes, take a sip and wonder what we were thinking just five years ago when we set up our will to give half of everything to Wil, outright. How naïve we were to think he'd go to college, let alone graduate. Did we really think he needed money as an incentive to pursue a four-year degree? Is that the space we were in when he was seven? I guess it was. The attorney's call just proves that to us.

It's not a lie, if you believe it.

There is a fine line between hopefulness and denial and we special needs parents straddle that line at all times. We push, we pull back, we dream, we adjust, we never give up, we surrender. We do all we can and when we can't do anymore, we sit on the couch and re-group until we're ready to go at it again.

When I picked Wil up from school yesterday, he pulled me aside conspiratorially and said, "Mom. We need to talk. We need to have Ava and Claire Rose over to jump on the trampoline. I can read their brains, and they are bored. They can come to our house and then they won't be bored."

I agreed and Wil turned to Ava and Claire Rose and said, "Okay, girls, go home, ask your moms if it's okay and get your swimsuits because it's going to be a sprinkler party at my house!"

I explain to the girls that Wil likes to put the sprinkler under the trampoline and jump in his swimsuit. It's about the closest he gets to swimming. Ava and Claire Rose agree, and scamper off towards home, promising to show up at our house very soon.

All the way home, Wil asks, "Mom. What should I wear to look nice for the girls? What snacks do we have for the girls? Will you get some towels out for the girls?" The girls, the girls, the girls...

Boy's turning thirteen in three months.

He's right on schedule.

The girls come, jump, eat, and laugh. A good time is had by all. When they leave, he says, "Mom. I really handled the girls well. I did really well having two girls here. I am good with girls. I think they had a nice time."

He's right.

Any girl would be lucky to have him.

But they'll never get him away from me.

CHAPTER THIRTY-TWO

Today, I was driving in my neighborhood and saw someone had printed off bright colored letters, slipped them into plastic sleeves, strung the sleeves together to form words, then hung them along a chain link fence. The sign said, "Hey, forgive yourself already." Just there in all its colorful glory - a sign, literally and figuratively.

For the most part, I don't walk around with a lack of forgiveness but I've got my share.

I just put Wil to bed and am grumpy and hurrying the process along. "You're not mad at me," he says, "you're mad at yourself."

Same message, twice in twenty-four hours - no accidents. After reading books and saying prayers, leaving on the light and promising to check on him every ten minutes, I make my way to my room and get ready for bed. I am tired. Am I more tired than just a day's worth of tired? Am I letting in some of the fatigue and anger and old stuff that I thought I dealt with in Sisters? It doesn't feel like that, it feels like maybe the sign and Wil were right: I have more forgiving to do.

Wil is almost thirteen. Is it time to say that he is who he is and who he is, is perfect? Should I have had an amnio? Done yoga during my pregnancy instead of being harried and exhausted from taking care of a two-year-old, laying my father to rest, settling his estate and moving? Instead of breathing the exhaust from living on a city bus line, should I have been sitting on a mountaintop taking mindful breaths? Even if there had been tests to show this child would have an autism spectrum disorder, attention deficit hyperactivity disorder and any number of other disorders, should I have taken them? Would it have made any difference? Would it have changed anything? How would knowing have helped when there's no question we would have continued with the pregnancy?

I think it's true what they say: ignorance is bliss. Perhaps while you can't go back to ignorance, you can choose to forgive: forgive the concurrent situations, forgive the ignorance, forgive yourself.

A couple days ago, Wil had me driving him to three different grocery stores looking for a Lifesaver popsicle. "Mom, do you think Big Safeway might have Lifesaver popsicles? I know Little Safeway didn't, but maybe Big Safeway does. Do you want to go to Big Safeway? Do you want to go now? Do you want to go to Big Safeway now and see if they have Lifesaver Popsicles?'

And so it went.

We tried Big Safeway, the "Little Store" and Plaid Pantry.

No dice.

On Sunday we went to four more stores: QFC, Fred Meyer, New Seasons and finally 7-Eleven.

God bless 7-Eleven. They had them. Individual ones with some serious freezer burn, but we bought up all they had, came home and put them away.

"Okay, I am going to be the ice cream man and I am going to sell the Lifesaver popsicles to you, Daddy and Jane. You are going to buy them from me and I am going to sell them to you because I am going to be the ice cream man. Don't forget. Promise you won't forget."

Then he got a bigger and better idea. "Mom, I am going to invite Keaton and Greg over after school on Monday. I want them to come to my house after school and eat Lifesaver popsicles. Go e-mail their moms and see if Keaton and Greg can come over. Go e-mail their moms right now and tell them to come tomorrow and eat Lifesaver popsicles that the ice cream man will sell them."

I e-mailed the moms and one mercifully e-mailed back within a couple hours that yes indeed, her son could come and "buy" ice cream on Monday after school.

The other mom didn't e-mail back until Monday morning

and I thought the planet might stop spinning such was Wil's angst over this loose end. But e-mail she did, saying her son could and would also come and "buy" ice cream.

People ask me all the time why I have pushed so hard to have Wil in a Catholic school when the public schools could give him more services. It's hard to put that long answer into a succinct response. How do I explain that I'm not looking for services... not that kind anyway. I'm looking for a community where an Elmo toting almost thirteen-year-old can get other almost thirteen-year-old boys to come and buy ice cream. I'm looking for a village of people that offer respect and dignity and love... nothing more than that and nothing less.

For weeks I've known it was coming: the anniversary of my father's death, June seventh. A man who didn't want his own grave but wanted to be cremated and buried between his parents. And so he is.

Yesterday was the thirteenth anniversary and through some psychological "trick," I "forgot." I didn't think of him all day long. It wasn't until this morning when I pulled off yesterday's page-a-day calendar and saw today's date that I caught myself.

It's amazing what we can block when we want to, at least in the mind. But the body always knows. And those around us. I felt a sense of ennui all weekend, a restlessness, a vague and nameless sense of ill-being.

But now it has a name: grief.

Thirteen years after the fact, it's not so much his death I grieve as his life. He was a tortured soul. It made him a challenge to deal with. But after his death there has been healing, understanding, forgiveness. As my brother says, "Dad and I are getting along really well now."

My father has come to my brother in a dream but didn't say anything. "He's not at a place where he can communicate yet, but he's getting there," my brother explained and I believe him. I haven't had a single dream about him. Yet. I know that soon I will and that our souls' journey together will move to the next level.

That will be something I will never forget.

The little studying of Buddhism I've done has turned me into a believer of reincarnation. I wonder if and when Dad is ever reincarnated, will he be born into a life that is lived? Will he be free from torture? Will he love who he is and who everyone around him is, completely? Will he be a person that feels he deserves his own grave? Will he, when all is said and done, be more like his grandson than his former self?

If my dad had lived to see and know Wil, I know that he would have been changed. My dad had a brilliant mind; he was educated at Stanford. I know somewhere in him there was a tender heart, too. I choose to believe that although their paths crossed on some other plane and not on this earth that that passing was big. Maybe there was some cosmic passing of the baton, my father handing his to Wil in the six weeks between his official death and Wil's official birth. Maybe my father said to Wil, "Wilson," my dad's surname for seventy-four years, "Here you go, boy. I lived my life from the neck up. See if you can live yours from the heart out."

Maybe.

I met with the teacher Wil will have for seventh grade next year. She's a great woman who taught Jane three years ago and remains Jane's favorite teacher ever. She also happens to have an adult child with special needs - thirty now - she gets it.

She asked me the kinds of questions we all hope a teacher will ask: "Tell me about Wil." "What are your goals for him?" "What would you like to see us work on this year?" Those kind of things.

Felt kind of silly just saying, "Love him."

It's not that we don't have "goals" but really, does the boy need to finish the year with algebra under his belt? Really?

She started telling me about a retreat the seventh graders would be going on in the fall. "We write down our regrets and burn them," she said.

"He'll need help with that," I said. "Not only will he have no concept of what a regret is, he won't have any. Really."

"Then we assemble a lunch for a partner - I provide all the makings for sandwiches, and the kids take each other's orders and then make the sandwich according to what their partner wants."

"He'll need help with that," I said.

The one-hour conference continued in that fashion. She with the "We..." and me with the "He'll need help with that..."

Later, Wil had Ed running up to Plaid Pantry to replace the package of Skittles he'd absconded and I agreed to ride along and run in for him.

I was telling Ed about the conference and he said, "You're starting to make me feel like the parent of a special needs child."

"I know," I said, "that's how I felt, too. The gap gets wider and wider each year. It's hard to even see the other side from here."

Just then we saw from our car windows a girl in a motorized wheel chair leave her home and head on down the sidewalk.

With no arms and legs.

None.

I'm seeing eights in my sleep. Spent the weekend looking for them.

Started on Friday. Jenn took Wil to Target during summer school time to play a game with prices, pretend shopping and comparative pricing - all good life skills he needs to work on. Didn't expect it to ignite a new obsession, but it did.

Saturday morning found Wil up and at 'em. "Mom? Can we go to Target and pretend shop? You will tell me to find something and I will just boom, run and find it. You will say, 'Wil, tell me how much Crest toothpaste is,' and I will just boom, run and find it."

Sounded innocent (and cheap) enough, so I agreed.

Don't know why or when the game morphed from boom, running and finding stuff, to boom, finding prices that ended with the number eight.

There are three prices that end with eight at Target and those are the red tagged clearance items so you have to keep your eyes peeled for those - and here's a hint, those are usually found on "enders."

If you're looking for nines? Veritable bonanza. Eights? Needle in a haystack.

Love Target. Love Jenn. Love Wil. Hate eights.

But here's the thing: I've learned that when you turn an eight on its side, it's the symbol for infinity. And while it felt like infinity when I was in Target being held captive by the obsessions of a nearly thirteen-year-old, it wasn't. It was more like twenty minutes. Thirty, tops. And while I have to remind myself that this too shall pass, no matter what it is he's currently obsessing over, what *is* infinite is his spirit, his joy, and his love. And you can't put a price tag on that.

CHAPTER THIRTY-THREE

Wil is thirteen! He is a teenager! For his birthday celebration we had my mom, Ed's parents and sister, plus the four of us get together. We sat outside in the backyard and for the third year in a row I made a pink cake with red frosting. He does not eat the cake but he requests it each year. So, I make it. I might say that's the single biggest gift that's come from being Wil's mother: letting go of the need for things to make sense, be "worth it." If he wants it and I can do it, it's worth it. This year for his birthday he wanted one and only one thing, a Touch-N-Brush, as seen on TV. He is the worst toothbrusher on the planet, but thanks be to the good Lord and fluoride, he has had only one cavity. I was all for something that encouraged tooth brushing.

So I bit.

I wrote down the 1-800 number and spent a good 30 minutes with a non-human, placing my order. When it arrived, I put it where I wouldn't forget it come birthday time.

He opened it among his other exciting gifts – college T-shirts to add to his three-drawer collection: Butler Bulldogs, Maryland Terrapins and Louisville Cardinals. He was thrilled. Actually? He was beyond thrilled. The party came to a screeching halt as Papa reached his 83-year-old hand in his pocket for a knife to help Wil immediately free the Touch-N-Brush from its cardboard surroundings.

"Dad, let's go put up my Touch-N-Brush. Let's go put up my Touch-N-Brush right now. Let's just go right now and put up my Touch-N-Brush."

For whatever reasons, Wil has adopted our upstairs laundry room sink as "his." So up went Ed and up went Wil and up went the Touch-N-Brush. Fortunately the thing is super simple (and quick) to install.

On his birthday night when I tucked him in he made me

promise I'd use the Touch-N-Brush before heading off to bed myself. I promised. I promised not to forget.

"Oh good," he said, "I could cry to high heaven - pretendedly."

Simple pleasures.

Simple.

Out of the blue, Wil had been asking to be taken to the Children's Museum -- a wonderful place designed for the preschool set. He often got dragged to the original location when Jane was much younger; it was one of her favorite places. We even had her fifth birthday party there. Don't remember him ever loving it though. Most of my memories involve trying to keep him in his back pack and handing snacks, pacifiers and bottles backwards, in a feeble attempt to keep him happy enough for Jane to finish doing her thing.

I think I once took both Wil and my friend's little boy to the new, bigger and better, location. They were three. Ten years ago.

Classic Wil, he pulls out a ten-year memory I have no knowledge of him having and wants to expand on it.

"Mom, I want to go to that place with the grocery store. I want to go to that place with the cash registers. I want to go and guess how much the food is. I want to make the sound beep when the food goes on it. I want to be the doctor. I want to be the ambulance driver..."

"The Children's Museum?" I asked, finally seeing the picture he was drawing for me.

Not answering, he kept up with all his big plans. "And Jenn will take me and we will bring Brandon and Sam, and we will play with the cash registers and the grocery store and the ambulance..."

Jenn would do that. She totally would do that, but I knew Brandon and Sam were far too old for the Children's Museum and that plan would not work.

So I begged Jane.

And she, being caught in a moment of feeling magnanimous, agreed.

So that's how on Thursday I walked into the Children's Museum with my thirteen and fifteen-year-old, and was asked politely by the woman at the desk, "Have you been here before?"

I decided it wasn't worth the long answer, so I just said, "Yes, we're here for old times' sake."

Oh, we got the looks. We got the "This is for *little* kids looks." The "Don't let your big kid wreck this for my little kid," look. It's okay. I remember being the mom of the little kid. I remember the protectiveness. I remember the fear. I remember the self-centeredness.

We ignored ninety percent of the museum in favor of returning over and over to the medical and grocery store sections. When Wil had had enough, we went to the snack bar and he got Nacho Cheese Doritos and water. Bliss upon bliss.

Holding my hand and skipping (literally - who knew the kid could *skip?*) in the parking lot as we wandered around looking for our car, he said, "Whew! I'm tired! I had a busy day! I was a grocery person! I was a cooking person! I was an ambulance driver! I was a doctor!"

"Yes, you were!" I overly enthused, trying to make up for my discomfort.

But inside I was thinking, *Best of all, you were a child.*

First it was Wil's desire to return to the Children's Museum, then he started asking me to help him count Volkswagen Beetles again. Each time we put one foot out the door he'd start in. "Mom, we are going to count VWs. We are going to find eighteen VWs. We are going to look until we find eighteen VWs and then we can come home."

Well ask and ye shall receive.

I'll be darned if we don't go out into the world and find the exact number of VWs he's after. They come out of nowhere. Seriously. It's comical. Just yesterday we drove less than five miles and saw twelve. Best of all, five of them were red, the preferred color.

Still needing to get six more in, I went in search of a big parking lot. It was a lovely day and we were exceedingly bored, so I parked and we got out. As is his habit (from years of screaming at him to do just this), he freezes by his side of the car and waits for me to come over and take his hand before stepping one foot away.

And so it was that we walked hand-in-hand throughout the parking lot on a just-right summer day, killing time, looking for (red) VWs.

Happy.

But then he said, "Mom? Can we find a blue two?"

Blue twos were something I thought we'd packed away and would not be bringing back.

But I was wrong.

Wil got braces yesterday.

Yes. It's true.

What's also true is that by Monday I may have lost my mind, along with my confidence in all the reasons behind getting the braces and the resolve to see this thing through.

Yesterday he went on a hunger (and fluid) strike and I saw the very real possibility this whole thing would end with a trip to ER. We did manage to get him to drink some water around 6:00 PM but the boy did not consume one single calorie from 6:00 AM yesterday to 4:00 AM today when he woke and was craving tuna fish.

Ed got up with him, mixed up two cans of tuna with mayonnaise liberally sprinkled the garlic salt and got him to eat both, drink a ton of water, and got him back into bed where he slept like an angel until 7:00.

Because he was able to put the mayonnaise laden tuna in his mouth and just swallow, he still has not chewed and announced, "I'll chew in two years when my braces come off."

It would be just like him to give up chewing for two years.

What was I thinking?

I *know* what I was thinking. I was thinking *I want him to have a beautiful smile. I want one part of him to not scream "special needs." I want one part of his adolescence to be typical. If he can't act like everyone else can he at least look like them?*

As I type this, my overly tired, highly emotional and couldn't-be-cuter thirteen-year-old son is two feet away watching some show on TV designed for preschoolers.

I feel loved and so does he.

Now.

All summer I've had a vacation planned, my idea of a vacation anyway; a trip to Sisters *all alone.* A whole week of just me, myself and I. Solitude. Silence. Serenity. My "you've almost made it through the summer" reward.

I've had a canvas tote bag sitting on the floor of my closet for two weeks. Every time I thought of something else cool to do on my vacation, it went in the tote: I Ching coins and book, Do-It-Yourself Tarot, a book on following the way of Mary -- a step-by-step pilgrimage, if you will. I was going to wake up in the high desert air after a uninterrupted 10-hour a night sleep, throw on a bathrobe to cover the chill from sleeping with the windows wide open all night and turn on the coffee. Then I would sit on my meditation cushion and do one woo-woo thing after another, after carefully recording my deep and prophetic dreams from the previous night.

Wil had been hip to the plan for weeks, even doing a big, "YES!" when I told him Jane was going to the lake with a friend for a week, I was going to Sisters and it would just be the three generations of men at home: he, Daddy and Elmo.

Saturday he was fine, then suddenly burst into tears, "I am sad you are leaving." He's never articulated his feelings so clearly and directly. That seemed to pass, so I continued loading the car and eventually left, arriving late afternoon in Sisters.

Sunday morning, I rose with the birds and was deep into

my various practices, basking in the fact there were six more days of this stretched before me. I was getting excited to go for a walk then coming back to do some *real* writing, after months of pretty much drivel.

Then Ed called. "We have a problem here. Your little boy misses his mom. He hasn't eaten anything since you left. He won't stop crying. I think you need to come home."

I threw everything back into the canvas tote, quickly made the bed, tossed food into an ice chest and hit the road.

So it is that Wil and I now have a week together that will be one thing, while I'd planned on another. It will not be a week of solitude, silence and serenity.

Instead, it will be a week of solidarity.

Ever since Wil got his braces on last Thursday, and stated he would "chew in two years," we've begun the soft sell which has worked for us in the past. We pick a date in the future and tell him that's the day he'll do _____. "Tuesday is the day you will chew again. Your teeth won't hurt, you'll be ready on Tuesday."

Usually Ed has the morning duty and I have the evening duty but as soon as Wil woke up Tuesday, he came to get me and wanted me to join him while he chewed.

I agreed.

Ed put a whole plate of tiny bites of garlic toast in front of him and he threw up a lot of roadblocks, "My body isn't awake yet," "I'm not ready to eat yet," "I'm not hungry." Finally Ed gently asked, "Are you going to chew today?" And he burst into tears and said, "I'm scared to chew." I finally got him to down a couple of Danimals liquid yogurt and we called it "breakfast." Then we moved as a unit into the living room.

I looked at Wil and said, "So, think of something fun for us to do today. We have the whole day back together, just us." Mr. Helpful (who, by the way, just *gained* a week of his life back) said, "How about the zoo?"

I replied with the ol' standby, "It's going to be too hot for the zoo."

Mr. Helpful said, "Not if we go early!" Then Mr. Helpful checked on-line and found that the zoo opened an extra hour early in the summer and we could leave right away to beat the heat!

Wil and I parked near the entrance, paid our exorbitant fees and I did a little self-talk. "Self? It's okay that you just paid twenty-four dollars to walk in the door and haven't even paid for the train yet. It's okay that you will likely see two to three animals and spend most of your time at the vending machines and drinking fountains. This is a rich experience for Wil that does not need the presence of actual live animals to enhance it."

I'd like to say the self-talk worked and to some degree it did, but every time we neared another animal and he veered me away, there was a *moment* of "oh, my God!"

At one point he was happily engaged at the vending machine and I needed the ladies room which was right there, so I said, "Stand right here, don't move an inch, I'll be right back. Oh, and sing, so I know you're still there."

I ducked inside and could easily hear him from the other side of the wall, "Glory to the God-est! Glorrrrrrrry to the God-est! Glory to the GOOOOOOOD-est!" I think that was the moment I stopped cursing Mr. Helpful's suggestion.

We eventually finished at the vending machines and bought two tickets to take the thirty-five-minute train ride around the zoo. We boarded the train. He made all kinds of "All aboard" and "honk, honk," sounds and Wil was happy as a sixty-five-pound clam.

When we got off the train, I could tell he was hungry so we left. In the car coming home he said, "Mom, my teeth should be in a good mood when we get home today."

"Does that mean you're ready to chew?"

"Honest to hell," he said.

When we got home, he chewed.

Honest to hell.

Worth every penny.

To say Wil is obsessed with ice cream trucks is akin to saying it rains a lot in Portland. One really has to live here and be wet nine out of twelve months for years to get it. For his entire life he's been fascinated by them. Then the fascination turned to obsession. Then the obsession turned to perseveration. From March first through October, it's "Mom, is the ice cream truck going to come today? Is it one hundred percent chance that the ice cream truck is coming today? Is it scale from one to ten, ten that the ice cream truck is going to come today?"

Approximately every twenty minutes.

And the songs. Dear Lord, help me with the songs. He hums, taps, and plays (loudly and often) on the piano "The Entertainer," "Do Your Ears Hang Low," and "Turkey in the Straw," all day, every day. ALL DAY, EVERY DAY.

For the last three months he's "been" the ice cream truck. He gets on his scooter, dons his helmet and away he goes. I follow along on Jane's old purple bike and stop him some pre-arranged number of times, always more than five and fewer than fifteen, most commonly twelve.

It is with great panache that I yell, "ICE CREAM!" every ten yards as we tool around the neighborhood. He pulls the scooter over, I pull the purple bike over, and I ask him for ice cream. My choices are: Sponge Bob Squarepants, Firecracker, Bubble Gum Swirl, Choco Taco, or Cotton Candy Swirl. When I've really had it and want to just mess with him, I ask for Mocha Almond Fudge to which he always looks quizzically and asks, "Do they make that?" Then he pretends to pull ice cream from the back of the scooter and slap it in my hand. I slap him pretend money and we're good for another ten yards.

Because I have far more pride and ego (and all the other deadly sins) than he, I try to only yell "ICE CREAM!" when we're out of earshot of passersby. Not easy to pull off, since our neighborhood has pedestrians everywhere.

All this is to say I've had it, he knows it, and that's what makes him our little Wil, doesn't it? Just when you can't take it another moment, he delivers.

Yesterday we went shopping for frozen fruit bars at 9:02 AM. He hummed. He tapped. He sang. He fiddled with every knob in my car. He went through my purse. He played with the windows. Just before my head exploded he looked at me with a thirteen-year-old boy smirk and said, "Want to hear the boob song?" Then he started singing, "Turkey in Your Bra."

This summer was a weird one. He got braces. He turned thirteen. And I think for the first time, he's become aware that he's different. He's cleaved to people, comfort items and rituals from the past as though his life depended on them, which I'm sure to some degree, it did. It does.

Labor Day Weekend he developed some weird swollen eyelid thing. Allergies? Infection? Something really awful? My mind went straight to worst case scenario, and I became completely obsessed. "My eyes are just swollen from all the crying," he said, when I asked him if they hurt.

You see he's been crying easily, too. He's cried more in the last three months than he has in the last ten years.

Something deep within him is shifting. It's more than puberty. It's more than the trauma of braces. It's more than just becoming aware of his differences.

He's not who and what he was.

He's not who or what he will become.

He's in transition.

I'm reflecting on this, trying to take it all in, trying not to get too lost in the what-does-it-all-mean-for-the-future madness, trying just to be with it, when he looks over the top of his glasses, shoots me a double dimple grin and says, "Mom, I need to admit something to you. I need to admit that I love you."

I offer a quick prayer to Mother Mary, "Thank you for always reminding me what matters, what doesn't, and that I am not alone. There is a plan, I just can't see it. It's a perfect plan and when I get scared and overwhelmed, I just need to admit that I am loved."

Thursday from 2:00 PM to 8:00 PM:

"Mom, tomorrow we will go to Fred Meyer at 7:00 AM. We will use the Self-Check. We will spend $35.35."

"Mom, if we buy three things for $10 each and one thing for $5.35, then we will spend exactly $35.35."

"Mom, do you think Swedish Fish cost $10 each? Should we buy three bags of Swedish Fish and one more thing?"

"Mom, wake me up at 6:45, I will just boom, get dressed, eat and brush my teeth, and we will go to Fred Meyer at 7:00 AM. Don't forget. Promise you won't forget. I can count on you, right? You won't let me down?"

Friday I awoke, ate, dressed and was just about to go get him when he woke up on his own (it's a rare thing for him to sleep that late, so I was sure I wouldn't need to "remember").

"Mom, I'm so proud of you for remembering! Good job in remembering! You didn't let me down! I'm so excited to go to Fred Meyer and spend $35.35! Let's get ready."

We were at Fred Meyer by 7:10. They open at 7:00. The boy needs new sweat pants as he's grown and his are too short. I thought, *perfect, that'll get us close, then we'll find one more thing and be out of here.*

We walked straight to the sweat pants, found a pair he liked in his size. $32.00.

"Look!" I cried. "Now we just need to spend $3.35!"

He was thrilled. We walked hand in hand through the deserted store and I cursed myself for forgetting a calculator. We roamed the aisles and I kept scratching out simple subtraction on the back of my checkbook deposit slips. One by one our possibilities were eliminated.

After about thirty minutes of this, it finally occurred to me that we could just buy the sweat pants and then buy a gift card for $3.35. Smugly, we proceeded to the Self-Check. We beckoned the one checker who was stationed in that area to help us "load" the gift card, and we swiftly swiped.

The sweat pants rang up for $22.40. The first time in my life I was unhappy to be saving a few bucks.

It took me longer to realize than I care to admit that I could simply increase the value of the gift card. The nice (and lonely) checker helped me void out the $3.35 and change the value to $12.95.

We walked out of there with the sweat pants, the receipt with the "right" number at the bottom (the only thing of value as far as Wil was concerned) and a gift for our friend Claire Rose's birthday, too.

As we held hands back to the car, Wil looks up, flashes the dimples and says, "Tomorrow we're going to try for $20.20."

Tonight is the night that Wil is having his first sleepover. He's never spent the night with a friend nor asked to have a friend here. About a week ago he was telling me about his friend Keaton's plans. "Keaton is spending the night with Greg on Friday and Michael on Saturday." He looked wistful.

"Would you like to have a friend sleep at our house sometime?" I asked, betting money he'd say no.

"Yes!" he said, "I'd like Keaton"

I contacted Keaton's mom. I explained the whole thing. I said it would need to be unconventional and because Wil goes to bed early and gets up early, a weekend probably wouldn't work for Keaton, but what about a school night? That way they'd only have a few hours together before bed and the next morning would be all about getting up and getting to school.

"Carrie," she replied, "I asked Keaton, he didn't even hesitate for a second. He'd love to come. He'll be there Monday at 5:00, right after he finishes his homework."

The boys are having a ball, laughing, eating popcorn, watching Monday Night Football.

I am watching them, feeling grateful.

On my bad days, I watch my son's friends move through the neighborhood as a pack without him, and I'm sad. They are laughing, joking, throwing a ball around, hanging out. He's back home hanging with Elmo.

On my good days, I'm thankful for this bunch of boys who are kind to him. They walk to school with him each day. They humor his quirks and laugh at his jokes. I know that even if they did ask him to join them as they roam the neighborhood, he'd say no. He's happy with how he's spending his time and does not feel left out.

On my bad days, I worry about the future. I worry about high school. I worry about what comes after high school. I worry about growing too old and too tired to continue caring for him but not trusting that anyone else can do it as well as me. I worry about what will happen to him when I'm no longer around to worry.

On my good days, I see how along every step of the path there have been angels. There have been people who didn't *need* to go out of their way to help, but did anyway. I trust that Wil's life is not an accident and he's been graced with an abundance of guides, both physical and spiritual, and he will be fine. He will be better than fine, he will thrive.

On my bad days, I list all the things that need addressing, all the changes that need to be made, all the goals that need to be accomplished, and a panic rises within me and threatens to snuff out my very life force.

On my good days, I list all the things we didn't think he'd ever do and yet is doing, all the ways he's surprised and delighted us, all the ways we've been so richly blessed by him and my heart is overcome with gratitude and appreciation.

On my bad days, I eat, breathe and sleep special needs. It's all consuming and I hate it and myself for falling into that trap.

On my good days, special needs takes its place in my life - a big place, but just a place; not my whole life. I am able to laugh, enjoy, and just *be*.

On my bad days, I'm wracked with scarcity: there's not enough time, not enough money, not enough patience, not enough help, not enough.

On my good days, I'm struck by the abundance all around me. All around him. All around.

I pull the car right up in front and he sees me as he files out of school with the rest of his class. He reaches for the back door, flings his backpack on the seat and scoots in next to it.

"Hi, honey, how was your day?" I ask, same as always.

Usually he says "Good." For all of September he said, "I'm tired," or even "Stressful," and the worst one, "Today was a day of hell." The last couple of days he's come home nearly skipping with an excited look on his face, and answered, "Great!"

"Can we go to Trader Joe's and buy more spinach pizzas?" he asks.

"Sure," I say, "I was just waiting to go until I picked you up so we could go together."

"Mom?" he says, and I prepare to receive his verbal list of all the other things he wants at Trader Joe's. But instead he says, "Why do I have braces? Why am I growing up? Why am I stressed out? Why am I not with you?"

Then he moves on to the verbal list.

"Mom, we need fruit leathers, too. And veggie sticks. And butter. We are almost out of butter."

For weeks, I've been tossing and turning over what's going on with him and what I can do about it. I had come to the same conclusion he had: he was struggling with his braces, with growing up, with stress and perhaps most of all, with separating from me. Not just transitioning from the summer to the school year, but from childhood to adulthood.

Today is my dad's birthday, October 8th. He would be eighty-eight today and that's something worth noting. I think about Wil's recent quest to find eights at Target. I don't believe it was an accident that he had that number on the brain right before this auspicious day. He is so tapped in like that. He knows before I do what there is to know, then he drags me kicking and screaming to the awareness.

There is a connection being played out between my dad, son and me. The little boy I was carrying while my dad lay dying is the boy who will work in his lifetime to break patterns, to heal the past and prepare for the future.

And I am in between, taking this boy to wherever it is he is going to go in life. Along his path. Healing my dad's path, and reframing mine.

For at least the last three years, Wil has declined all offers to get a new Halloween costume, instead opting to wear the red M&M costume we bought at Goodwill for $1.50 a million years ago. It's comfortable. There is no mask. It's predictable. It's red. It's perfect.

As soon as we turned our calendars to October he started in. "Mom, the Halloween carnival is on Friday, October 30th. I am going to wear my red M&M costume and Claire Rose is going to be a green M&M.

In the back of my mind I made a hazy note to check in with Claire Rose about this, but I kept forgetting.

Finally, about two weeks ago I saw Claire Rose when I picked up Wil from school, and I said, "Wil tells me you are going to be a green M&M with him for Halloween, is that true?"

"Yes! I am!" she chirped.

I put the whole matter in the "handled" section of my life and forgot about it entirely.

Until.

My friend liz (she insists on a lower case "l") who is a teacher at school, came by on Thursday evening so we could go have dinner. She said, "Claire Rose is trying to get a hold of you. She is wondering about the green M&M costume." That's when it dawned on me that Claire Rose thought I had it and I thought she had it.

I knew it was not a matter of going to the store and buying another one. I haven't seen them for sale in years and I could see Wil's simple dream going up in smoke. Not an option.

I racked my brain until I remembered that Kathleen's daughter had been not only an M&M one year, years ago, but I thought a *green* one. I called Kathleen's cell phone. Yes, she thought it was green and she thought it might have survived her recent purging of the costume box, but she had a distant memory of lending it to someone and couldn't remember getting it back. She'd check when she got home.

liz and I went off to dinner and about the time the wine arrived, Kathleen called. The green M&M costume had been located - she would put it on her front porch for me so I could get it on my way home and take it to Claire Rose.

And that's just what we did, except when we got to Claire Rose's house she wasn't home. I feared she had her mother out searching the town in vain for a green M&M costume. I tried calling her cell phone but nobody answered. About an hour later, Claire Rose called.

"Carrie? Did you try to call?"

"Yes, Claire Rose, I wanted to let you know I found you a costume and I put it on your front porch. I hope you aren't out looking for one right now."

"We were picking up my sister from soccer and then we were just about to go looking for a costume. Your timing is perfect."

No, Claire Rose, you're perfect.

And Kathleen, you and your daughter are perfect, and liz you are perfect, too. You are all part of this perfect plan to help me raise Wil. There are no accidents and there are angels everywhere.

Wil's praising of the Lord is so loud it wakes me up. "Table of plenty, table of plenty, come to the table of plenty" he sings. And sings. And sings. And plays on his electronic keyboard. And piano. And drums. And recorder. And harmonica. And every window of the house. And door. And kicks to the beat against the breakfast bar.

Ed says, "Look at his joy. Such joy. We are so blessed. How long do you think it would take a stranger to become annoyed," he asks, "two days? Eight hours? What do you think?"

"Fifteen minutes," I say.

To Wil I say, "God, you're cute."

He puts his face right up to me and says, "Looks like you're talking to God when you say I'm cute."

And he's right.

CHAPTER THIRTY-FOUR

I'm a routine girl. Give me a routine, let me stick to it and I'm a happy girl. I'm out of my routine during this l-o-n-g winter break. Way out. So far out I can't see my routine from here. This happens every vacation break and I fight it every time. But this time I'm trying something new. I'm trying to detach from my routine, knowing it will be there waiting for me in seven (short!) days and I'll be able to pick it back up and cloak myself in it soon enough. In the meantime, there is a *new* routine to accept - the no routine, routine. The one where instead of doing laundry and emptying the dishwasher as my compulsive nature would so glory in, it has me playing Mario Kart on the Wii with Wil before I've even had breakfast. It has me not making any plans so that I can go with the flow of the day as it unfolds, instead of forcing a clock on a day that has no sense of time. It has me walking by rooms that need cleaning, rugs that need shaking, gifts that need to be put away and counters that need wiping. It has me walking away from what doesn't even matter in the scheme of things, and straight into the arms of what *does.*

Wil looked at me yesterday after we'd been hanging together, spontaneously made the sign of the cross on his forehead, chest and shoulders while saying, "Cross my heart and never die, mother of Jesus."

I would have missed that if I'd been anywhere but right there.

I find myself turning back to his words again and again, "Mother of Jesus." I have, perhaps, an unusual relationship with Mary, ever since my dad made a weird proclamation one drunken night, years ago when I was a child. "You're the next Virgin Mary!" he shouted. I've been scared of his threat. I've been avoiding what it may have meant to him, and certainly what it could mean to me. Now, after hearing Wil's words and having spent the last thirteen years being forced into a new relationship with God, what I think about God, and just who I even think of as God, I think we are all called to be the mother of Jesus. Mary was a human that answered the bell. She said yes to God knowing there would be unbearable sacrifice in one lifetime, and from that sacrifice, eternal blessings for all of humankind. Am I a mother of Jesus? Am I a Mary-like person? I am certainly a mother of a child who is here to teach, to lead, and to love. I have that in common with Mary. I hope that's not all.

I'm not a dog person. I would have a cat in a minute, but all three other inhabitants of this home are allergic. So, no cat.

Dogs need walking. Dogs have muddy paws. Dogs shed. Dogs like to lick you and rub up against you and I'm not a touchy-feely kind of person. I like my personal bubble and it's generous in size. Dogs invade my personal bubble. My personal bubble is all that keeps me on this side of sane some days.

The other inhabitants are dog people and would love to have one. I get four votes to their three, however, as we all know to whom responsibility for a dog would fall. And so, we do not, have never and will never get a dog.

Right?

So on Tuesday we're sitting with Dr. Willis, and he asks, pointing at Wil, "Ever think of getting this guy a dog? This guy needs a buddy."

As I protested, he smiled knowingly. He listened to my many, many, many reasons why we could not possibly get a dog, and he said, "You're right. But the right dog would take ten percent and give ninety percent. The right dog would make your life easier, not harder. The right dog would free up your time, not create more work for you, especially if the dog was Wil's responsibility."

Dr. Willis suggested a Labradoodle both because of how smart they are and the no shedding thing. I didn't even know there was a no-shedding dog. Brilliant. I told him I knew of a family with both a special needs boy about Wil's age and a Labradoodle. I would talk to them about it and agree to consider a dog.

Just consider it.

The very next day I pick up Jane from school early and we head over to New Seasons before picking up Wil. We run into a dear friend of ours, Candace. She was Jane's eighth grade mentor for a special independent learning project. We're chatting it up in the narrow aisle of New Seasons and who walks in? Patty, Jack's mom, the one with the Labradoodle.

I say to Patty, "I can't believe you just walked in the door. You're on my 'To Talk To' list. Wil's doctor wants us to get him a Labradoodle."

Patty proceeds to give me one hundred and one reasons why that is a fabulous idea. Candace says, "That's the kind of dog we have, too!" I can't believe it, as I've seen both dogs and they look nothing alike. Then I'm informed of the three different sizes and how Candace has a mini and Patty has the largest size. Plus, there are lots of colors and variations and for anyone like me -- with an untrained eye, they look like different types of dogs.

Within twenty-four-hours of the discussion with Wil's doctor, I discover that two of the most invested-in-our-family friends have Labradoodles and love them! There are no accidents.

So Candace says, "There are two great places to get Labradoodles in Oregon. We got ours from Labradoodle Angels."

Jane exclaims, "Angels? Mom, you collect angels! It's a sign."

We eventually say goodbye to Candace and Patty when Jane says, "Mom, it can't be an accident that we ran into both of them at the same time and they both have Labradoodles."

So we go home, I dump Jane, am getting ready to head out to get Wil and she calls out from behind her computer, "Mom! Guess what? Guess what one of the puppies is named?

Guess!"

"I don't know," I say, "Jane?"

"No! Mary! M-A-R-Y! It's another sign!"

And I'm sure it is. I'm sure Mary is messing with me again. And I've agreed to go down this path a little further, warning everyone involved that I reserve the right to turn around at any point.

I then remembered another thing Patty said to me, "If you can get over the shedding, you should really talk to Claire. She places retired guide dogs, or guide dog trainees that are dropped from the program for various small reasons. 'Career change' they call them.

Hmmmmm, I thought, *it would be great to get a trained dog instead of a puppy and one that comes built in for service!*

Again I swore to Patty and the universe, "I'll think about it."

Last night, Ed and I went to a fundraiser at Jane's school and I hadn't made it ten steps in the door before I ran into Claire. I never see her -- even though we live in the same neighborhood -- and there she was.

"Carrie!" Claire said, "I hear I'm supposed to talk to you about dogs!"

"Oh, I see you've already talked to Patty!" I responded.

"Yes! And I won't try to talk you into it because it really is a huge commitment but I do have to tell you, I have the perfect dog for you. She's a small black Lab - only fifty-two pounds. She just retired, but she's only five or six. We don't usually retire them until they're ten or eleven. She's super sweet, super mellow and used to go to school every day with a child. She won't be hard to place and there are people with higher priority on the list, but they don't have kids and I really want to place her in a home with kids, ideally with special needs."

"What's her name?" I ask Claire, wondering even as I say the words why I'm even asking because asking will only bring attachment and I do not need to become attached to this idea, let alone this dog.

"Flicka," she says, "like the horse! Are you too young to

remember 'My Friend, Flicka?'"

"No," I tell Claire, "I remember that book and movie. I can't believe that's her name, because Dr. Willis told us we needed to get a buddy – a friend, for Wil. Maybe this is a sign."

"Just call me Monday or after you've had some time to think about it," Claire says, "but don't take too long, she'll go fast – she's perfect."

I walk back over to join Ed, Jim and Kristen. "That was Claire, she talked to Patty, she has a dog for us," I say.

"Claire? Claire was here?" Jim says. "We've adopted two dogs from Claire and are on the list for a third. They are the best pets. You should totally do it!"

I look at Ed. Ed looks at me and a look passes between us that says, "Looks like we're getting a dog."

I'd been thinking a lot about this dog that's been retired from the Guide Dogs of Oregon. I found myself welcoming this dog into our home, into our family, into my heart. Already. Found myself thinking of the logistics and coming up with hair clean-up strategies that are reasonable and not OCD.

Somehow a dog that wasn't even a consideration a week ago is now something I'll be really disappointed about if it doesn't happen.

I called Claire on Monday and she said I needed to complete an on-line application. So I did, within the hour. Now it's been a few days and I haven't heard back from the agency. Still, I am resting in the knowledge that if not *this* dog, then, *a* dog. A dog for Wil. A dog to help us. A dog for us to love.

I wrote an e-mail to Patty, "Just how many Mary candles do you have going over there? We're getting some serious get-a-dog ju-ju over here."

She wrote back, "Mary is screaming at you, I hope you're listening."

I'm listening.

Of course, Wil is the least excited of anyone about the

whole idea. I asked him in the car on the way to get Jane after school, "Wil? Do you even *want* a dog?"

Clutching Elmo he piped up from the backseat, "On two conditions. No peeing on the floor, no barking, and no biting." I didn't bother to correct him. I got the point. The boy is a little scared of dogs and frankly, so am I. I assured him we'd get a trained dog that would not pee on the floor, definitely would not bite and would not bark unless there was danger. He was satisfied.

"Okay, then. What's the dog's name?" he asked.

"Well, there is a dog named Flicka, but we aren't sure we'll actually get that one. She might go to another family. We don't really know yet."

"Is Flicka a boy or a girl?" he asked.

"Flicka is a girl," I answered, hands on the steering wheel, eyes meeting his in the rearview mirror.

"I will have a boy dog. I will say, 'Here, boy.' If we get a girl dog, I will call him Flicker. We will have a boy dog named Flicker."

Flicker. That's what I have of hope. That we will do this. That this is meant to be. That Mary knows what she's doing here.

Wil asks, "Mom? Will the dog come to school with me?"

I look up from my book and say, "Well, I don't know. I'm not sure you'd need the dog to come to school. Why?"

"Don't dogs go to school sometimes?" he asks.

"Yes, sometimes they do, for people with disabilities."

"Do I have a disability?"

"Kind of," I answered and immediately regretted that non-answer answer.

But it satisfied him.

And it kind of satisfies me.

CHAPTER THIRTY-FIVE

We have Flicka! Two weeks from the day Dr. Willis suggested we get a dog, we got a dog. No, we did not get *a* dog, we got the perfect dog. She is mellow. She is sweet. She is perfectly trained. She already knows that she is Wil's, Wil is hers, and there is already some serious love going on.

We met Claire out at Guide Dogs for Oregon and she had Ed, Jane and me stay back while she and Flicka walked towards Wil. She then gave Wil the leash and the three of them took a walking tour of the campus, the three of us walking twenty paces behind just taking in the view. If I weren't already a believer in reincarnation, I would be now. There is no getting around the fact that Wil and Flicka are picking up on an existing story – an old one. They have karma and it is a thing of beauty.

Wil feeds her, carefully measuring her food from the cup Claire gave him. Wil keeps track of when she needs to go outside and "do her business." At night he puts her on her bed right beside his and they lie down and fall asleep… together. Dr. Willis was right. Wil needed a buddy. How could we not have seen that? He is such a social boy and as the developmental gap between him and his peers grows wider every year he needs a buddy who thinks he's all that and a little bit more.

I didn't realize how badly Wil needed a companion nor how much I would enjoy one. Preferring solitude over pretty much anything, I surprise myself by how much I enjoy having Flicka snooze along side of me as I work at my desk, lie on her blanket in the kitchen as I fuss in there or just greet me like the queen of the universe when I come home from being gone briefly. And here's another thing that has surprised me. I've enjoyed brushing Flicka to help with the shedding. We hear Labs shed profusely two times a year and then a little all year long.

"It's the undercoat that sheds," Claire had warned. "You have to get it with a Shedding Blade, but be careful not to hurt her. Get a bag and capture all the hair or your whole yard will be full of hair - enough to clog the lawn mower."

Flicka lies down happily on the warm concrete. I brush and brush and brush and brush. It is rhythmic. It is soothing. It is peaceful. It is, dare I say, *healing.*

Her undercoat is definitely shedding. She is losing what she is no longer in need of. She is done with it. The spring is coming and she simply has no further use for it. And she is smart enough to allow someone else to help her take it all away, gather it in bunches, stuff it haphazardly in a bag and dispose of it.

I want to shed profusely twice a year and a little all year long.

Today is Ash Wednesday and I have the black smudge in the shape of the cross on my forehead to prove it. I went to the children's Mass at Wil's school today and slipped in the back. I sat by myself even though I knew ninety percent of the people sitting in the large, sunny church.

This, for me is a time of quiet... this forty-day period marked with ashes to commence it with Easter as the culmination. I could use a forty-day quiet period. Ask any of the people that have to live with me and they'll tell you. I'm wound far too tightly and as much as Flicka is a calming presence, I need more. I need forced quiet. I need external boundaries set on me that insist I take it down a notch or ten, and enter into a reflective period.

The church was packed and there were four stations to receive ashes and later to receive communion. Although I was baptized and confirmed in *a* church, I am not a member of *this* church and thus, I do not receive the blood and body of Christ. I receive a blessing. I have a "thing" about the blessing. Unless I am seated in the section that is going to end up going in the priest's line, I just skip the whole thing. I don't want some *regular* person blessing me. Besides, Father Chris is so special and when I do go through his line he stops what he's doing, lays his big warm hand over my whole entire head and says my name. Then he delivers a fresh and personal blessing and I swear to God, I can feel the blessing pulse from my head throughout my body as this holy man says the special words he's chosen just for me.

Today, however, after choosing my place of isolation in the back I was not going to make it into the priest's line. When I looked up to see just who *was* doing the communion for my region, it was Patty. I thought, *why not?*

I was the last person in the whole church to go through any of the lines, everyone was either on their way back to their pew or down on their knees waiting to wrap it up. Patty might have very well wanted to give me the standard blessing in the name of time but Patty is not that kind of person. She is Holy with a capital H. I met her when her son, Jack joined Wil in third grade, making them forever Wil-and-Jack; the two boys in the same class with special needs. My guess is that Patty was always a wonderful woman, and from what little I do know about her past, that seems to be the case – always one to walk her faith, to help others, to give generously with her time and talents. However, I think it was Jack that made Patty holy. When you have a child with significant needs, those needs either make you or break you. They either make you bitter, or they make you holy.

As I stood before Patty, she laid her hands on me and said, "May the blessings of the Lord be upon you." Then she reached over, grabbed my whole neck towards her and into an embrace and said, "ALWAYS."

One word made all the difference.

"Regular" people are capable of bestowing pretty awesome blessings.

May the blessings of the Lord be upon you.

Always.

Just came home from another pre-evaluation meeting to

update Wil's IEP – individual educational plan. Because we are now having him evaluated - educationally- for autism spectrum disorder, we've had to start over from scratch. Just calling and saying, "Hey, could you add one more thing to the evaluation?" doesn't fly. You have to meet again, say everything you've already said, stammer in all the same places, look around the table hopelessly for someone to jump in and rescue you, then go home and fall apart. All over again.

Today, I feel like I know nothing, have no answers, have nothing but a bleak future to look forward to, and really, have made one poor decision after another.

But that's just today.

And that's the nature of bureaucracy. And the nature of being a small cog in a very large wheel. And the nature of parenting in general, maybe. I don't know.

I don't know where Wil will go to high school. I don't know what Wil will do or where he'll do it after high school. I don't know what will happen to Wil, where he'll live and what he'll need as an adult.

I don't know.

And that's the difference between special ed. parents, we know that we don't know. Nobody knows, but we *know* we don't know.

And that's a powerful knowing.

I know that Wil has his own sense of knowing, however, and that comforts me a lot. Just a few days ago, I picked up Wil and his friend Ian from school for a play date. They have been friends since kindergarten and every couple of months Wil reports, "Ian wants to come over - been awhile since he's been here." And so, Ian's mom and I get our heads together and make it happen.

So, on a day when Jane was otherwise engaged I took the two boys out for ice cream. The three of us sat round the table, Wil tapping, humming and kicking happily while Ian and I visited.

"Wil won a water bottle today!" Ian tells me excitedly.

"Oh, yea?"

"Yea, it was Walk + Bike to School day and everyone that walked got to enter a raffle for a Nike water bottle. Wil turned to everyone at the table and said, 'I know I'm going to win that water bottle,' and guess what? They called his name! He *knew* it!"

Wil continued to eat, kick, hum and tap, unimpressed with his own powers.

And that's just one of the things that make him so impressive.

Two mornings in a row, I've awakened from nightmares involving Flicka. It reminded me of when I was a new mother and I dreamt I'd left the baby somewhere or went to the closet to get a pair of shoes and there was the baby in a shoebox.

Two nights ago, I dreamt I walked into my dad's house, the one he died in nearly fourteen years ago and opened the freezer in his garage. There was Flicka. She was fine, despite the fact that I was the one that had shut her in an airless freezer and forgotten all about her.

Last night, I dreamt I suddenly realized I'd forgotten all about Flicka and she had been locked in my car for twenty-four hours straight - no window rolled down, no food, no water, no potty breaks. I went running to the car when I finally remembered her and some family was picnicking on the grass alongside where my car was parked. I then noticed someone had picked the lock on the car and one of the back doors of the car was open. Flicka had been let out by a stranger; a concerned, well-meaning stranger. When I found her she was happily lying on the backseat waiting patiently for me.

What part of me have I put in the freezer (deep freeze, even), perhaps as long as fourteen years ago?

What part of me has not given myself enough oxygen, food, water and breaks, and has required that well-meaning strangers come and provide me the access to those? Although Wil's needs no longer consume me entirely, it would still be hard for me to define where he leaves off and I begin. We are fused. There is a natural progression mothers of "typicals" go through as their teenagers exert their own will and desire for independence. The moms must deal with that. Some deal with more skill than others, but deal they must. Their child is growing up and they must change their relationship accordingly. When you are raising a child that is perpetually a toddler not making any moves towards increased self-reliance, not capable of being left alone, not on the track for living independently – ever – what's the point of separating?

Wil and I are going to actively be in each other's lives until one of us draws our last breath. There is no "until he's eighteen." There is no "until he gets married." There is no until anything. Although being fused may not be the healthiest way to go through life, to some degree it's a matter of necessity. But so is self-preservation. I must continue to put myself on the list so I can walk the planet hand-in-hand with him for many decades to come.

CHAPTER THIRTY-SIX

"Mom, let's go to the park and play basketball and then let's go to Dairy Queen and get a milkshake."

It is a gorgeous spring evening and so I agree to his requests. He runs upstairs to change from his uniform into basketball clothes. We get the calculator which he will hold in his right hand and use as a scoreboard and a big red and black basketball to hold in his left hand. We drive to his designated park even though three parks are within walking distance of our house. He finds a court, Flicka and I find a spot in the sun and we find a bench on which to watch, wait, clap, cheer and help sing at "halftime."

We have two quarters, there is no telling him that when you divide the game into two you end up with halves and not quarters, there are always two quarters, never four. "Mom, we'll have an eight and a two," he shouts over at us on the bench as he takes a few warm-up shots.

"A real eight minutes," I say, zipping up my jacket all the way to my chin - there's a sudden breeze and I can already tell I'm going to get cold sitting here if his "eight" turns into a twenty.

He dribbles, shoots, scores, calculates, coaches, plays the fight song and is the on-air commentator for the greater part of twenty minutes. "Let's not be in a hurry," he says, reading my mind. "When we're done, let's swing on the red swing and then do the tittie-totters." I fight the urge to tell him fourteen-year-old boys should not be saying tittie-totter, but instead agree to not be in a hurry.

Meg Hutchinson's song, "Hard to Change," has been running through my head for days; the lines, "I can barely hear you, over these machines, turn them all off, and tell me 'bout your dreams," loops through my brain and I look over at Wil. He's forced me to turn off all the machines and just be with him, "not in a hurry."

"Mom, when we are done we will go to Dairy Queen and get a small vanilla milkshake with a long red spoon and we will not be in a hurry to drink it. We will sit there and we will not be in a hurry. We will just sit there. You will not be in a hurry. Don't forget. Don't forget to not be in a hurry."

Meg's lyrics cycle back around, "Want to hear the silence in my life, but I bought all these tools to save time, well if they save so much - then where's all mine?" What's the point of having high speed Internet, DVR, answering machines, cell phones, etc., if I don't have time to watch an "eight and a two" basketball games and sit beside my beautiful son on a plastic bench and watch him drinking a small vanilla milkshake with a long red spoon?

"Mom?" he looks up at me between bites, "we're having a double date."

And we did.

Jane and I are taking a yoga class from a Lithuanian woman. Not enough has been made of how disparate the amount of time is that I spend with my two children. I often tell people I have two only children, their needs, their interests, their abilities, their everything, makes me more of a plate spinner than a mother, just keeping both their lives separate and moving forward is the goal. Yoga is my latest attempt to do something just with Jane, hoping to snag a few Wil-free minutes on the way to and from class, perhaps stopping at the next-door bakery for a cookie when we're done.

I love the yoga teacher's heavy accent and actually find it helps me to focus as I have to work so hard to understand her directions. She throws extra letters into her words, heart becomes hearlt. Roots becomes rloots. Sitting becomes seating. I love her and everything about her.

But as much as I love her, I want to fly completely below her radar. I want her to notice me not a bit. I want to come in, lay down my mat, disappear, and when I am done, leave. I don't want her to come over to me and help me readjust into the correct position. I don't want her to tell me with a bright smile, "Yes! This is it! Beautiful!" like she does with the others. I don't want her to have an opinion of me or my efforts and this neurosis is just one of the many reasons I've stayed clear of yoga for many years.

Today we walked in, almost sneaking into the studio and had almost made it entirely through the class escaping her notice entirely. We were in Savasana - relaxation pose, also called corpse pose - I was home free. Nothing to do but lie there and breath, I mean, how can you screw up corpse pose?

Over she comes, grabbing my ankles and tugging on them gently. "Give it to me," she says. I open my eyes (corpses have their eyes closed), and she is looking at me with such tenderness it is more than I can humanly bear. She nods, repeats, "Give it to me." I "give it to her," having no idea what "it" is, but I make every effort to Raggedy Ann my legs and let her move them wherever is she sees fit. I think I'm done. Eyes closed, I breathe, relax and suddenly she's at my temples. "Give it to me," she says.

I think it was a matter of a language barrier. I'm sure she was talking about my tension, trying to say "let go, relax," but there's something much more powerful in the phrase, "give it to me" than there is in the command, "relax." It's as though she were asking me to turn all my worries over to her - if even for a moment.

Maybe she was. Maybe I should. Maybe.

There was a time when I really believed Wil would catch up. Developmentally delayed meant just that to me: delayed. I see now that he will never be caught up, and that's okay. He's where he is, and where he is, is perfect. Where he is going will be revealed. All will be well. Not better. Not worse. Just different than planned or hoped for.

One of the things the school psychiatrist who recently evaluated him got stuck on was his trouble in answering what he wanted to do for work when he grew up. I, frankly, thought he'd say a garbage man or ice cream truck driver, but apparently he said, "I want to be a dad."

"Yes, but what will you do for work?" she persisted.

"I will work with my kids," he said.

"Yes, you will work with your kids, but what will you do for a *job?*" she badgered.

"I will be a stay-at-home dad," he said, realizing she wasn't *getting it.*

When she told me that story, I had to wonder which one of them had the communication disorder. He will work with his kids. Period. That's work. I love that not only does he know that, it's what he wants as his vocation. I couldn't be prouder.

I am aware that Wil has an autism spectrum disorder. I am aware that might make being a parent, let alone the one that stays home, difficult, if not impossible. I am also aware that Wil has a solution in place.

"Mom, when I am married and have five sons you will live with us and you will help me with the boys. We will have a van and we will take the boys in the van to Dairy Queen every day. We will get vanilla milkshakes with red spoons. Don't forget. We will just say, 'Come on boys, get in the van. Let's go get ice cream!' Don't forget mom. Don't forget about the van. Don't forget to help me with my five sons."

As a woman who quit "working" when Wil was three and made the raising and advocating for him my life's work – never to retire, I appreciate his answer. I will fight the urge to argue with people who don't get it, who don't think being a parent is a job. I will not waste my time telling them that for me, and apparently for Wil, there is no higher calling.

Wil tells me every single night when I tuck him in, "Don't forget to leave your door open."

I don't forget. I keep my door open. Every night. I reassure him repeatedly.

And still, I got a note the other day from him in his large, all-capital letter writing, "LEAVE YOUR DOOR OPEN, MOM. DON'T FORGET". Made me think… *what "door" could he be talking about?*

I think the "door" might be Catholicism – they say what you resist, persists and that is certainly the case with me and my journey to find a spiritual home. I don't want to be just one thing. No one religion can hold all that I believe and I long to be part of a community in an official capacity. I want to be part of something and perhaps being Catholic can be part of what I am, if not all of me, then a part. I've never before considered joining the Church and being okay with the fact that it is not all that I need, all that I believe, or all that represents me, but a part. A shade of grey in my black and white spiritual world.

Somewhere around the third park of the day, I began to settle into it: this is my life. Thought it would be one thing and it is quite another. I didn't imagine spending my days going from park to park to park with an almost fourteen-year-old to watch him awkwardly play with three and four-year-olds while discerning if we are actually getting funny looks or if I was just imagining it.

When he wasn't on the play structures, we were looking for drinking fountains. Four parks, seventeen drinking fountains; each one sipped from once, twice, three times.

Miles we covered and my mind and soul fought with each other with every step: I should be folding the three loads of laundry that sit on my bed right now. I should be wrapping Mother's Day gifts. I should be vacuuming dog hair. Cleaning bathrooms, spending time with Jane, with Ed, returning a call to a friend, writing a card to my friend about to have major surgery, returning e-mails, fixing dinner, reading the book for book club, grocery shopping, changing beds, should, should, should. My mind said I should be doing anything and everything but being right here in this moment. This perfect moment.

Wil is going to keep dragging me to parks until I stop

fighting it and am one with it. That's his job. To make me conscious, line me up, to bring me to the center, to connect me to the Divine.

On Sunday, we were walking back from the neighborhood school playground and we ran into a friend of mine, Paige. She has a child on the spectrum and although our boys don't know each other, we know all about each other's boys. You know how that goes. Wil asks her, "Did you see the ice cream truck at your house? If you see the ice cream truck come by make sure you tell them to come down to our house. Don't forget. Promise you won't forget."

"Well," she says, "you know my boys have a lot of food allergies, so sometimes I get the kinds of treats they can eat, put them in an ice chest in the wagon and we walk around passing those out to the neighbors."

That's all it took.

"Mom? Can we go to Paige's house and get ice cream after school? Can we go to her wagon? Can we just go there right after we pick up Jane and just go straight there and get ice cream?"

Relentlessly.

So, Monday I e-mailed Paige and asked if we could swing by and would it be possible that Wil give her a dollar for something she had in her freezer.

She e-mailed back and wanted to know just *what* it was he liked. What was the *exact* song he preferred the ice cream truck to play, etc. When we pulled up to her house at the designated time (3:45) she had the wagon all out, had made a big sign to put on the outside displaying all the kinds of treats they had (and that she'd driven all over town shopping for) and as we got out of the car she grabbed her iPhone, pushed "play" and out came "Do Your Ears Hang Low?" Who does that?

Then, because she'd created a monster and the weather here is downright wintry this week with unbelievable rain, she has taped the sign to her car and driven to our house three days in a row at Wil's preferred ice cream eating time. She even lowered her prices, $0.05. Truly, those popsicles and that friend? Priceless.

Tonight Wil wanted to go to the playground and I heard myself agreeing without a grumble - something just went off in my head that said... *this is important.*

Got there and immediately ran into two friends, one being Paige, the ice cream truck lady. The other, a man I've known since Wil was born and now he too is the parent of a special needs child.

I had Flicka sitting next to me and kids kept coming up to me and asking if they could pet her. Next thing I knew a little one asked if he could take Flicka on a walk. I said sure, and got busy solving the world's problems with my friends on the bench. Occasionally, I would look up to make sure Wil was fine and that Flicka was within sight and doing okay with her new role as Pied Piper. Each time I saw her she had gained another follower. One would return Flicka to me and then the next would ask for a turn. We finally established a little routine, a route, to make it fair. They could each take Flicka once around the loop, bring her back to me and then it would be the next person's turn.

I was aware that a young dad had two kids, a boy about four and a girl about two, now in line for Flicka. The little boy had a Scooby Doo Band Aid on his cheek and when I asked him about it, he awkwardly touched it. The dad said, "Marty, ask what the dog's name is." The boy didn't ask. "Ask how old the dog is," the dad prodded. The boy didn't ask. "Ask if you can pet the dog, Marty." The boy didn't ask. I didn't think too much about it. The dad and I got to talking and I told him Flicka was a retired guide dog. He marveled at her beauty, her shiny coat, her sweetness, how young she looks.

Suddenly, Flicka was up on the play structure so I jumped up to get her down - can't have her scaring the kids up there. All the followers were trying to get her down and there was some degree of temporary chaos. The dad followed me. Once down, I turned to the dad and said, "I think Flicka was checking on Wil. He has special needs, you see, and that's why we got her. She knows she's his buddy and she was probably worried that she hadn't been with him for awhile."

I saw the look in the man's eyes. *The* look. The look of one that walks the path. "*Your* son has special needs? *My* son has special needs. Did the dog just automatically know that she was there for your son? I can tell she understands my son, too." I told more about the story of Flicka and how yes, she knew she was there for Wil, and that their bond was a thing of beauty.

We chased kids and dogs, passed the leash, made small talk, and then I asked, "So, what's going on with your son?"

"Well, we're just finding that out now," he said, giving me *the* look again and smiling a little too broadly.

"It's so hard," I said, making eye contact with him and noticing tears behind his eager smile.

"Yea, looks like he has dyspraxia, sensory processing disorder, maybe autism... does your son have any of those things?"

"Check, check, check!" I said.

Our conversation went on and he said how he wished his wife could meet me as she is desperate for other mothers to talk to about things like this. I told him about the support group I run and that his wife is welcome to join us. "Oh, that would be so great," he said about four times.

"I don't have anything with me to write down my information, do you?"

"No," he said, "but do you come here very often?"

"All the time," I said.

I have no doubt that Wil, Flicka and Mary will make sure our paths cross again.

And I'll have a pencil and paper when they do.

I'm feeling like it's being revealed to me why Wil is so insistent that he, Flicka and I go to the park every night: we have work to do.

Wil performs his magic on the play structure, delighting the four to eight-year-old set, and Flicka makes it possible for me to meet people I would not otherwise meet.

The other day, Wil and I couldn't find any other kids to play with at Park number one so we walked down to Park number two. There was a mom and her daughter swinging on the only two swings. Wil and I took the teeter-totter. Soon the little girl left the swing and came over to us. That turned into her teetering her seven-year-old self with Wil's tottering nearly fourteen-year-old self and me trying to balance the two out with some degree of success.

Off the teeter-totter and on to tag, the mom and I were left to talk. She started asking about Flicka and the next thing I knew, I was telling her all about how we got her. That story has a couple of versions, the just-the-facts one, that's not bad, really, and the woo-woo one complete with every no-accident-detail. I went for version number two.

"That's what happens when you put it out into the universe… the universe rises up to enfold you," she said.

I knew I'd found a friend.

We talked for two hours. Wouldn't you know it, my "New Friend" has a child with special needs. We eventually moved back to park number one when Paige called to say she'd brought the ice cream "truck" down there. I introduced my "New Friend" to Paige and after I left, they did more talking and sharing of resources.

The other day, I was at park number one and I noticed something going on with each of the kids who were chasing Wil in a rollicking game of hot lava monster. All these years, I've been bringing him to the park thinking he was the only one with special needs and just assuming everyone else was neuro-typical.

Can't believe this far into the game, I still don't have the Make No Assumptions "thing" figured out. One thing I *have* figured out is that Wil, Flicka and I will continue to go down there and play as long as there is a bench to sit on.

And to listen.

My dad died just a few weeks before Wil was born and nine years before my nephew Kunga came along and yet, there is no denying my father's role, his presence, his spirit when you get these two "brothers" together.

Kunga has been dreaming about my dad lately, waking up and saying he misses him. He spontaneously told both Jane and me this, too.

"I miss my granddad," he said.

"Do you remember him?" I asked.

"Yes. I remember him."

"Tell me about him," I pressed.

"I didn't *know* him, he died before I was born, but I *remember him,*" he clarified.

And there isn't a doubt in my mind that he does. Nine years together on some other plane is hard to forget.

Wil, who had to be told by a five-year-old that his shoes were on the wrong feet said one profound thing after another this weekend, as we spent our time in my father's old house, where my brother, his wife and son now live.

Ed simply asked, "Hey, Wil, what time is it?"

"You'd know if you had harmony in your soul," he said.

After playing with a ball in the back yard, Jane said, "Wil, where did the ball go?"

"I affected your energy and now you can't find it."

My dad was a piece of work, but after fourteen years only the fond memories come to mind now when I think of him - there's been time to heal. The "brothers" only know the funny stories, and there were plenty. They have a divine connection to a man that is their grandfather, a man that affected their energy.

A man whose soul has finally found harmony.

Amen.

"Mom, after school let's go to the park and play basketball," he said while eating breakfast.

"Okay," I said.

"Mom, after school let's go to the park and play basketball," he said while brushing his teeth.

"Okay," I said.

"Mom, after school let's go to the park and play basketball, "he said while getting dressed.

"Okay," I said.

"Mom, after school let's go to the park and play basketball," he said while making his bed."

"Okay," I said.

After school we came home and I said, "Are you ready to go to the park and play basketball?"

"I need a break first," he said, going to his computer, turning it on and proceeding to type gibberish madly while talking to himself.

"Okay," I said.

I busied myself doing laundry, checking e-mail, putting dishes in the dishwasher. Finally, he yelled out, "I am ready to go to the park now!"

"Five more minutes," I yelled back.

"Mom!" he exclaimed, but then went back to typing manically so I thought I'd dodged a bullet.

Then the phone rang, the dog needed to go out and the clothes that could only be dried for ten minutes were ready to be taken out and hung up. Five minutes had turned into fifteen. I feared trouble as flexibility is not Wil's middle name. Going with the flow is not the game around here. Re-adjusting is not something that comes easily.

"Okay, I'm ready now, " I said. We put on coats, shoes, got the leash for the dog and stepped outside. Pouring rain. He looked at me uncertainly.

"Looks like we waited too long, now we're going to have to make another plan. How about we play with the soft basketball in the living room, instead."

"Okay," he said.

I've waited nearly fourteen years for this day.

I had a check to deposit and Wil likes to use the ATM, so off we went.

He punches in my PIN.

He punches in a series of yeses and no's, and finally we come to the amount to deposit. I am holding the check; he hasn't laid eyes on it.

"Put in $72.36," I say.

He stalls.

"7-2-3-6," I repeat.

He doesn't move.

"What's wrong?" I finally ask.

"I'm going to put in $72.35," he says.

I start to argue, not wanting to enter the wrong number and mess everything up, but get the urge instead to re-examine the check.

Wouldn't you know it… the check was for $72.35.

Friday, Wil decided he wanted to meet Paige and her two boys at the park at 2:30 PM. He also decided he would like the ice cream truck to happen to be driving by at the same time so he had me text Paige while he went to put three dollars -- one dollar per boy -- in the pockets of his basketball shorts.

I texted Paige and said, "We're headed out the door, if it works to come right now, we'll see you there."

Didn't hear back.

We got three houses down the street and what did we hear? "Oh, Susanna," not only the ice cream truck but the preferred song.

We plunked ourselves down in the nearest shade and waited for the truck to come closer. We've learned the hard way that trying to chase it is an exercise in futility. We waited about two minutes and it turned the corner and came down the street we were on. We waved it down, were just making our way over to it and who should drive down that very street at that very time, but Paige with both boys.

Wil looked at them with no surprise on his face, only

relaxed certainty as if to say, "Oh, good, there you are, just as I'd planned."

The boys enjoyed their treats.

The moms enjoyed their visit.

The universe enjoyed the trust and faith of one special boy.

CHAPTER THIRTY-SEVEN

Wil turned fourteen on the fourteenth of this month – his golden birthday. Went shopping for paper products for his party: plates, napkins, that sort of thing. Found the Elmo-themed stuff and grabbed it. The boy does love Elmo... actually has a stuffed Elmo that he calls his son. Upon closer look, I saw that the Elmo party pack was just like the one I bought him thirteen years ago, "For baby's first birthday." So, I put it back. Couldn't do it. Love the boy, would do anything for him *except* get him something that says that. Not that he'd care. But I care. He is not a baby. He is fourteen and while he may not want nor need any of the things that a typical fourteen-year-old wants or needs, he is not a baby.

Went to a different store and found an Elmo balloon. Had the young man at the counter help me blow it up, attach a matching red ribbon and weight, and loop it through my cart to finish my shopping. Saw three babies in the store point and make sounds as they saw Elmo flying high in the air of Safeway.

"Where'd you get the Elmo balloon?" one heavily tattooed young man pushing a stroller asked me. "It's my son's first birthday today. He loves Elmo."

"Over in floral," I answered. "It's perfect for a baby's first birthday."

"Exactly," said the man.

Then I went home and cried.

And got ready for the party.

And wished my baby a very happy birthday.

And it was.

Happy birthday, Wil! Fourteen years ago today you were born - on your due date - big and healthy and full of life. I love you now and always, Mom

Wil had a great golden birthday - full of love. He got phone calls, e-mails, texts, and drop by visits. Plus, gifts. Lots and lots of gifts. A dear friend Nancy, gave him fourteen dollars (all in ones) for the ice cream truck - he was thrilled. He got a great baseball cap, a new bike helmet, and a lot of little things wrapped up simply for the joy of opening (think: toothpaste and hand sanitizer).

Claire Rose came by with a stuffed Cookie Monster and a card that said on the front, "Happy birthday, you were born for a reason. God picked this time and place for you to live your life because he knew there were so many lives you would touch.... Inside the card said, "And today I am just grateful to be one of them."

I was outside watering in the backyard when Claire Rose came to the door. By the time I got around to the front he'd already opened the card. Claire Rose looked at me, "You're gonna really love the card I gave Wil, Carrie," she said.

She was so right.

So often I forget how great it feels to do something all by myself. It's so hard to teach Wil to do things for himself and so hard to be patient as he tries, and so hard to resist jumping in to make them go faster, easier, cleaner.

But.

Every year, a few months before his birthday, I start brain washing him about the next big hurdle he's going to cross when he turns a year older. One year it was riding a two-wheeler. Last year, it was taking a shower (instead of a bath - a big deal due to his Sensory Processing Disorder). So for the last year, he's showered, but I've helped. I've washed his hair. I've dried him off. I've picked out his pajamas. I've put the dirty clothes in the laundry room, hung up the towel, shut the shower curtain. Basically he stood in one spot and sort of rubbed soap on himself.

Now, for the last few months I've been telling him that fourteen-year-old boys need to completely shower by themselves - no mothers allowed. And they need to shower every single day. Last night he did the shower and hair but wanted help drying off (crossing the midline is still a huge challenge).

Tonight I said, "Wil, it's time to go upstairs and take your whole shower by yourself. I'll be downstairs waiting for you and when you come back down I will flip my wig five times." (Something I said once inadvertently and it has stuck - he's loathe to miss a wig-flipping opportunity.)

Darned if the boy didn't run upstairs, get himself a clean towel, shower, wash his hair, dry off (sort of) put on clean pajamas and come back downstairs in under five minutes! (The hanging of the towel and subsequent trip to the laundry room will be tomorrow.)

I can't tell you how proud of him I was.

But the best thing of all was how proud he was of himself.

Truth be told I do not wish Wil were "normal," I love him the way he is and he is *our* normal. Normal isn't a place I live or even want to live.

But I wouldn't mind a visit now and then.

We're up early, filling ice chests, grabbing blankets, sunscreen, hats, flip-flops, and sunglasses. It's as much work going to the beach for the day as for the weekend, but we don't do weekends at the beach. We do one day trip a year, same beach, same activities, same everything. For Wil. He looks forward to it all year long.

"Did you program the DVR? We want to make sure our show records," Ed says.

"Got it," I say.

We pile into the car, Flicka and Wil in the back row, Jane and her pillows and iPod in the middle, Ed and me in the front. We drive the ninety minutes to the Oregon Coast, leaving the ninety-five-degree day behind and head into fog and a thirty-degree drop in temperature. Relief.

We head straight to the arcade, load our plastic cards with

credit and begin swiping. First on the list is "Wheel of Fortune," but that one machine is out of order as is the Gatorade machine, another top attraction for Wil. He is not deterred, the show will go on. We move throughout the should-be-demolished building and find "Deal or No Deal." Two dollars a game. We play several. Magically, tickets come pouring out of the machine as Wil makes, and does not make deals. He's offered one hundred tickets in exchange for his one remaining case. Two boys, about ten, standing behind him watching (and waiting for the game) shout, "Deal!" Wil says, "No, I don't want one hundred tickets, I want two hundred tickets."

Wil slams the No Deal button and we all groan. He then is instructed to open his last remaining case. Two hundred tickets. As one hundred tickets come out of each of the dispensers by his legs, the boys in line look incredulous. Wil sees their faces and is more excited that they are excited than anything. "Want my tickets?" he turns and asks the boys? "You can have one hundred each."

They gladly take the tickets.

We gladly leave and go to the beach to set up.

We spend the day throwing a football, playing with Flicka in the water, eating snacks and watching the sand TV.

Deal.

Wil and I walk into Safeway hand in hand and we immediately see Carmen. Carmen has worked there forever and definitely all of Wil's life. She's seen him at every age and state. "Hi, Wil," she says.

"Hi, Carmen," he answers.

"Boy, you're getting so *tall*," she declares.

"Yep. I'm 5'2" now," he continues.

"Are you excited for school to start?"

"Yes," he says looking her *in the eye*.

"Have a great rest of your summer, Wil!" she says as we push the cart through the aisle.

"I will," he says.

He puts one arm around my neck, the other hand pushing the cart along side of me.

"Wil?" I say, "that was a really nice conversation you had with Carmen. I didn't have to tell you one thing to say, you did the whole thing!"

"That's because Papa knows how to roll!" he says, referring to himself with one of his many self-named nicknames.

Roll, "Papa," roll.

CHAPTER THIRTY-EIGHT

Father Chris is back! He's been on a leave and we've all missed him terribly.

Ed, Wil and I hold hands and walk out of Mass. "I'm ready to sign up," I tell Ed.

"What? Did I hear you correctly? The dyed-in-the-wool non-Catholic? Did I just hear you correctly?"

"Yep, I'm ready. And for all intents and purposes we are already members of this church. We've been coming here more and more in the last twelve years. We don't want to go anywhere else. We don't want to be a different religion or denomination. We are part of this community and we intend to remain so. It's time to stop dating the Catholic Church and commit."

"Let me see how you feel after the welcome back Father Chris glow has faded," Ed says.

I let his comment pass. I know how I'll feel in a few days, a few weeks, a few months and a few years. Ready. Ready for something that I've been inching towards for my whole life. It started with the weird and disturbing, "You're the next Virgin Mary!" comment my father made, and continued with his fears that if I went to a Catholic high school I'd "end up marrying one of them." It has not stopped since. It's not rebellion. It's not a process of elimination. It's a calling… a calling to be part of something bigger than me. Something that is flawed. Something that has far to go in many respects. Something that I can only agree with in part, but in large parts, important parts. Like a marriage, the commitment is to a work in progress and there will be flexibility, faith and forgiveness required throughout.

I'm ready.

In the car coming home from school on Friday, Wil pipes up

with, "Mom, Jesus Christ is coming back you know."

"Where has he been?" I ask, one eye on the road, the other in the rearview mirror.

"Hell," he says with a laugh.

"Oh, yea? Where is he going when he comes back?"

"He's going to live in our hearts this time."

He prattles on and I nod and give him the occasional uh huh. I think back to the book I've been using for my morning prayer time, *Living Buddha, Living Christ* by Thich Nhat Hahn. I think back to the days when I was the last person to bed and the first person up. I did mornings with both kids. Now I don't even do the Wednesday mornings I was doing after I got home from Sisters that summer almost four years ago. I simply don't do mornings at all now. Ed does them and he does them well, happily. And I instead, spend up to an hour in quiet prayer and meditation on a cushion before an altar in my closet. Also in my closet is a coffee maker and small refrigerator. I make my perfect cup of coffee – just one, not several, as in years past, and sip it mindfully. I read from books, say my prayers, count my blessings and quiet my mind before walking out of the closet and into my day.

Today I read what Thich Nhat Hahn said about the importance of Sangha – community -- and that to have your spiritual roots be in more than one religious tradition only serves to strengthen your connection to the divine – not weaken it. That's how it feels to me, too. Although I am now committed to becoming Catholic, am excited in fact and don't have any second thoughts, that doesn't mean I want to stop learning about Buddhism or any other world religion. I want many deep roots that hold and sustain me. Although everything that I believe cannot possibly fit into the box marked "Catholic," that is truly where my Sangha – community – practices their faith, and after bucking what was right in front of me all these years, I no longer want to buck, I want to embrace. I want to be part of something bigger than myself in a concrete way. I want to sit on a pew, hold hands as we say the Our Father and wipe tears from my eyes as we celebrate baptisms, communions, confirmations, marriages and yes, even deaths. Together.

Kathleen and I continue to walk together four mornings a week – we're in our twelfth year. She knows Ed and I are going to join the Catholic Church and that we're asking for Wil to be baptized. She doesn't know that I am going to ask her to be my sponsor. Arms pumping, legs marching, winter cold all around us in the early hour, I ask her, "Would you like to be my sponsor? I know you have a million things going on and this is just one more thing. This is a big commitment – every Wednesday night for two hours, plus all of Holy Week. How do you feel about that? It's okay to say no."

"I would have a big problem not being your sponsor," she says. I take Kathleen for granted the way I take breathing for granted – she is just always there for the taking, always there to breathe life into my dreams and bolster the inevitable heartbreaks of life. She has tutored Wil one morning a week since first grade. Free. She has heard my rants and loved me anyway. She has heard my raves and loved me anyway. She's endured my phases, watched as I've let people come into my life who I shouldn't have and patiently listened as I processed the need to kick them out – and loved me anyway. She's never judged, never lost patience, never lost faith that I would eventually pull my head out any number of times. In short, she has been a living Christ. And not enough can be made of that. A silent, patient, persistent, ever-present Christ-like being right in one's own backyard, or more specifically, to my right four mornings a week for twelve years.

Wil has been asking to go to Tom and Nancy's house in the afternoon since last spring. It started innocently enough, they have a great swing on an impossibly tall tree in the backyard and he loves to swing on it. At first, we'd walk down on a beautiful day, swing, and leave.

Then it turned into him doing a bit of a concert and singing church songs at the top of his lungs in a falsetto voice. Nancy would come out from her kitchen and we'd sit around the patio table and visit. If Tom happened to be home, he'd join us, too.

Then our visit got extended and we'd stay for a beer (me) and water (him). Then snacks became involved. Then, every now and then turned into him obsessing and begging to go every single day, which Nancy and Tom graciously accommodated as much as their busy schedules would allow.

Spring turned to summer and as summer turned to fall we thought the trend might die out. No. We just moved the party inside. Tom put away the patio table and chairs and instead of bringing Flicka and hanging in the backyard, we took over their family room. Soon Wil decided there was more action in the basement where there was a computer, big TV, an extra fridge with things Nancy bought just for him and even his own secret hiding place for his snacks so no one else in the family dare eat them).

Fall turned to winter and things got busy with the holidays. We still made it over there two to three times a week, though. Then Nancy's dad got really sick and was in the hospital. Wil had a hard time understanding how it was more important for Nancy to be at the hospital each day with her dad than being in her basement waiting on him hand and foot. "Nancy's dad is really sick, Wil, he might die. Nancy needs to be with him."

He got quiet, thought about that a minute then asked, "Does everyone die?"

"Yes, honey, everyone dies."

"I'm not going to die, I'm special," he said.

"There's no question you're special," I said.

I don't know if he's just heard the term "special needs" so often, or if he thinks he truly will beat death, or that he understands that there is no beginning, no ending, only everlasting love and that those that live in that love live eternally.

I'm betting on the latter.

CHAPTER THIRTY-NINE

We are meeting with Father Chris to work out the particulars of joining the church. "After twelve years of dating the parish, we are ready to get married," I joke. He laughs. There are rumors that he may be leaving soon. Frankly, this is a concern and one reason why we are hoping to speed this thing along: we need to be made Catholic before he leaves. The next priest may not be cool with the two rows of Buddhist prayer flags that line our porch. The next priest may not be okay with the fact that we're not making Jane join, too, and that we really haven't had all that many conversations with Wil. The next priest may not be okay with the simple fact that even though I will at last call myself a Catholic, in my heart that will always be a little c catholic, meaning universal.

We meet one Thursday morning in early December. Ed and I walk in and Father Chris embraces us in one of his famous bear hugs. "Welcome," he says, "or should I say, welcome home?" The man is downright giddy. "I have been smiling ever since I got your e-mail. This is just great. Just great!"

He motions us into a little room in the Parish Center where we can all sit around in chairs and talk easily. I spill my beans, "I am ready to be Catholic but it will never be all that I am. I cannot take everything I believe in and put it in a box called "Catholic," there will always be other religions that I want to learn from, other spiritual practices I will want to incorporate into my own. It will never be all that I am but I'm happy to include it in the list. "Like what?" Father Chris asks with genuine interest, not judgment.

"Like the Eastern religions, especially Buddhism," I answer.

He smiles and says, "Did I tell you the story of my nephew, the yogi?" He did preach about him but the story is good and so I say, "Please tell me."

"My nephew spent months with a group of Buddhist monks. He marveled at their ability to smile every day, all day long. Finally he said to one of them, 'Tell me the joke,' he just could not get his arms around the fact that a group of people with 'nothing' had that much to smile about. He gets it now. I do, too. What else? Rumi? Do you read Rumi? I love Rumi!"

The conversation went on for an hour with Ed partaking, too, and all three of us coming to the warm conclusion that joining the community in which we were already heavily invested was not only timely, but ultimately blessed.

"You will just join the RCIA (Reconciliation of Catholic Initiation for Adults) group in January. Ed, didn't you already do half a year a couple of years ago? So really, you will just be putting those two halves together, you won't miss much at all. Carrie, tell me more about your Catholic journey."

I tell Father Chris the story of my dad finding out I was going to go to Marist – the only Catholic high school in Eugene, and him saying, "Don't go marrying one of them! I'd rather you married a black than a Catholic!" I told him about my Baptist minister grandfather and the belief I grew up with that praying to Mary was worshipping a false god. I told him that it took me nearly 48 years to get over those voices in my head and hear my own.

"Truly, it is Mary that brings me to this decision, however, and I haven't been able to find her anywhere but in the Catholic Church." I say to Father Chris, to Ed, to God, to the universe. "My father once told me I was the next Virgin Mary." That felt like a curse, not a compliment. I ran from that pronouncement all these years. I now have come to understand his rant better. I think all women are 'the next' Virgin Mary. I see virgin as meaning pure. I think we, women, are all called to a purity of heart and for many of us it comes only from the extreme sacrifices of motherhood. We don't know true love until we've given birth; until we have experienced a love so real that at last we really experience love.

When I was a little girl in Sunday school we made banners one time that simply said, 'God is love.' I felt like that was a riddle. Wasn't God, God and love, love? Wasn't love something you felt, maybe even something you *did*? How could that *be* God? Instead of asking someone to explain it, I just looked at the burlap fabric with felt letters hanging from a chopstick each time I descended the steps to our basement. Now I'm glad that it took me years and years to get that, and that I didn't have it explained to me. Even if someone had explained it perfectly, love is inexplicable. God is inexplicable. If we're lucky someone or something comes along that points us toward an understanding and from there we follow the bread crumbs to a belief in something that makes us feel settled in our souls. And that is love. And that is God, and as my favorite artist, Corita Kent says, "You are God and you are not God. Do not get the two confused. It is one."

On Wednesday nights, Ed and I go to the Parish Center, sit in a circle with three other adults going through RCIA plus one going through Confirmation. It's perfect that it's on Wednesdays because Wednesday is the day of the week that Ed started going to Mass in the mornings - halfway through his week, putting balance into his life that had been dominated by mind and body. Wednesday mornings also brought balance back to our equity at home, moving me into the position of morning sub, from CEO of mornings.

I have asked Kathleen to be my sponsor and Ed has asked her husband Jerry to be his. We feel a little like we cheated, coming in mid-stream into a group that's been journeying together since September and now it's early January. For Ed, it's really just finishing what he started with a two-year "recess" in between. For me, it's also finishing what I "started," if there even is a start to a faith journey. And if there is a start, where is mine? With my Baptism as a child? With my first understanding of God? With my first rejection of that and subsequent wrestling match? I think faith is circular, not linear – just like grief it moves in concentric circles and feels at times like you're back where you started, but really, you've just moved through another layer.

It's super special doing this with Ed and although it took us twelve years of being part of this community and nineteen years of marriage, I very much feel like we are at an important beginning of the "new us." My summer in Sisters was almost four years ago, when I was forty-four. Four is the number of elements: earth, fire, air and water. Four is the number of seasons. Four is the number of labor and stability. We have labored for four years to redefine and recreate our marriage and there is stability to it that wasn't there before. Maybe it's God. Maybe it's being two middle-aged adults, instead of two egocentric young kids. Maybe it's having nearly fifteen years of raising a special needs child and nearly seventeen years of being parents. Maybe it's watching our own parents age and seeing one set of them in a stable, long-term marriage, and one set of them... not.

What takes it from being super special and puts it in a whole other league is doing it with Jerry and Kathleen, two people who have a marriage, while not perfect, that's as warm and loving as any I've ever had the privilege of witnessing. They are truly each other's best friends and biggest cheerleaders. Jerry travels a lot for work, some years as much as fifty percent of the time and when they were raising three small children, that took a toll. "Still," Kathleen once explained to me, "there is always a longing for the other one."

I'd never thought about longing for anyone really, but I love the idea of that, of being so "married" that when you are separated from the other -- even just for the day, there is a longing to come back together at the end. I can already see that deciding to go through this RCIA process together is bonding us in a holy way.

One of many reasons we decided to join the Church is that Wil is in eighth grade now and will soon be leaving the school. We don't want him to leave the community. In fact, we want the community to continue to embrace him and if need be, support and love him long after we are gone. We didn't really give Wil a chance to decide if he'd join the Church, too. We just told him, "Wil, you, Daddy and I are joining the Church. You will start going to classes after school – just a few, and your friends will be there, too." That was pretty much it. We worked it out with Father Chris and the Religious Ed. person

Vicki, that two of his biggest angels -- Ian and Claire Rose -- be sponsors for him. Vicki agreed. Ian agreed. Claire Rose agreed. We talked to Jane about becoming a Catholic and she said, "I don't want to be just one thing." That was hard to argue with and although I don't want to be "just one thing," either, look how long it took me to reconcile that.

"Are you okay with Dad, Wil and I joining, and you not joining? Will you feel left out?"

"No," she said.

"We will ask you to go with us to Mass on occasion, but for the most part it will be your choice to partake or not."

We talked the whole thing over with Father Chris and he felt strongly that to talk an almost seventeen-year-old into doing something she didn't want to do would backfire. I want Jane to have a guilt-free process of choosing her own spiritual path – whatever it may be.

Wil is being Baptized and receiving his first Holy Communion today. Wil started his march towards receiving these Sacraments this winter and enjoyed the process tremendously. Loved the other kids in his class. Loved the sponsors (fellow eighth grade students, many of them), loved the teachers, loved the teacher assistants, loved it up one side and down another. "I will miss RCIA," he said. I think he'd like to go every other Thursday from 3:30 to 5:00 for the rest of his life – and my wheels are already turning on how I can get him to be an assistant for next year's class going through.

Of course, I worried. Worried that he would not put the host in his mouth for the First Communion (with the entire church looking on). Worried that he'd freak out at the cup. Worried that although we were assured by the priest (repeatedly) that he would only "sprinkle" him and not "dunk" him, that somehow he'd get too wet or worry about being too wet and again, freak out. Worried that our non-Catholic family would be uncomfortable being in front of the whole church as Wil received his First Communion, and knew it would break his heart if they weren't there. Worried for months. Sent one thousand e-mails. Got consoled one thousand times. "It'll all work out," I was told over and over.

"I will take the host, but I will not drink the wine," Wil told me repeatedly. "I am fourteen. Fourteen-year-olds do not drink wine." How was I supposed to argue with *that*? Nonetheless, when it dawned on me that he was the only one receiving First Holy Communion today and all eyes would be on him, I wanted him to take the cup. Ian saved the day, "Hey, Wil, just fake it. Take the cup up to your mouth, but don't take a sip!" Brilliant. Then I sent up a prayer that the person "assigned" to hold the cup would be our principal, who totally gets him.

And of course, all the worry is in vain. He is not in the least bit freaked out. He is pretty much rocking it. Fair to say, there isn't a dry eye in the place when after we -- his parents, godparents and the priest -- anoint him with oil, he gives a big ear-to-ear grin and flashes us with the thumbs up sign.

It only goes up from there. Father took Wil's success very seriously and thought of details I could not have thought of. "I will have Ian and Claire Rose join him in the font. I will have them help me baptize him. I will do 'In the name of the Father,' then they will do the Son and Holy Spirit."

Father helps him up out of the font and he stands on the ledge, facing out at the congregation. The music leader begins to sing and play on his guitar the "Alleluia Chorus" and Wil raises both his arms high as if conducting an orchestra. Pure joy is on his face. When the music ends, Wil makes a point with his right index finger, flings his right arm out at the congregation and finishes with a big "AMEN!" There is laughter. There is applause. There are tears, and I'm afraid some ugly crying too, from me.

Later Ian says to me, "That was the closest I've ever gotten to crying tears of joy."

Then there were all the other things I should have thought about and totally didn't. Not to worry. Kathleen thought of asking someone to come and take pictures. Two brilliant photographers come and capture the whole thing. And of course, the principal comes up to me right before the Mass and asks, "Did you assign anyone special to be Eucharistic Ministers?"

"I was hoping *you* would be," I say, then I tell her about Plan Fake. She makes the necessary arrangements and there she is. "Amen," Wil says, clear as a bell when he receives the host from Father. Then he moves over to the principal and does a great fake, after which, also clear as a bell he says, "Did I fake it?"

The eighth grade moms take it upon themselves to plan a little reception afterwards in the classroom. I don't lift a finger. I just show up and get to bask in the glory.

Ed, Ian, Claire Rose, Wil, his four godparents: Kathleen, Jerry, Tom and Nancy and I process out with Father. It's very emotional looking around the church at all the people that love my boy. Not just like him. Not just put up with him. Not just being nice. These people love him. Kathleen turns to one mom after we're almost to the back of the church and asks, "What did you think?"

She answers with tears in her eyes and a warm smile, "That that's what it's all about!"

I asked God for an easy baby. I couldn't handle one that cried a lot. God gave me Wil and taught me patience along the way.

All the way along Wil has brought me gifts I did not ask for and forced me to re-think the ones I have.

Through Wil I have learned compassion, empathy, tenacity, unconditional love, gratitude, and faith.

Wil has shown me what it's like to be ego-less. He has helped me inch away from the goal of a perfectly clean home to the goal of a perfectly clean soul.

Thank you, Wil, for being my greatest teacher, my wise, funny, forgiving, consistent, persistent, and ever-loving guide.

Amen.

ABOUT THE AUTHOR

Carrie Link has contributed to *Rose & Thorn Journal, Fearless Nest: Our Children as Our Greatest Teachers,* and *The Complete Guide to Hiring a Literary Agent.* She has written a monthly piece for the "Hopeful Parents" blog since 2009. Carrie has been blogging since 2006. Her blog "love." chronicles life with her special son. Carrie lives in Portland, Oregon with her husband, children, and her amazing community. She can be found at http://carrielink.blogspot.com or carriewilsonlink@gmail.com.